SURE SUCCESS IN ENGLISH GRAMMER, TENSES, ASPECTS, ARTICLES AND LETTERWRITING
Copywright © Onye kingsley 2014

All Rights Reserved

No part of this book may be reproduced in any form by photocopying or by any electronic or mechanical means, including information storage or retrieval systems, without permission in writing from both the copyright owner and the publisher of this book.

ISBN 978-0-9569415-7-2

First Published 2014 by
KINGSLEY PUBLISHERS (UK) LTD.
76 Foxcombe Fieldway Addington Village
Cr0 9ez,
Croydon
London.
www.kingsleybooks.co.uk

Printed for KINGSLEY PUBLISHERS.

Table of Content

Tense and Aspect	Page 2-4
Use of pronouns	Page.5-15
Punctuations	Page.16-22
Grammatical Function & description of words.	Page.23-27
The Clause	Page 28-30
Figure of speech.	Page.31-36
Writing Skill, Essay, Letter, Article, Compositions.	Page.37-101
Hints On Summary passage. Use of common Foreign utterances in	Page.102-129
English Language usage.	Page.130-135

TENSE AND ASPECT

TENSE:

Tense is one aspect of grammar that makes many teachers and learners of English language to wonder. There are up to 16 tenses traditionally in English as of today. Nevertheless, linguists have seen through this traditional flaw-that is the traditional grammarians equated "tense" with "time" every race has three 'times' namely, the <u>present,</u> the <u>past</u> and the <u>future.</u> Hence "time" is a universal concept.

Vice versa, tense is the form that a verb takes to show the time of an action. For this reason, there are notably two tenses in English that –is "present" and past tenses".

i.e.

get - got

drive - drove

work - worked

go - went

see - saw

This means that 'get' is the form that the very "to get" takes to show the present time, whereas 'got' is the form that indicates a past action. There is no form of the verb that indicates a "future event" as a result there is no future tense in English.

ASPECT

Aspect, people often mistaken for sub-tenses'. It is (aspect) a form or category of the verb that shows duration, inception or continuity or completion.

There are two aspects in English language, these are:- 'progressive aspect' and perfective aspects. Progressive aspect is indicated by a form of the verb 'be' with a present participle as in <u>is singing, was singing;</u> perfective aspect combines the form "have" plus a past participle as exemplified by <u>has / have /had taken.</u>

The disparities between tense and aspect can be seen below:-

	Present tense Progressive aspect	Present tense Perfective aspect	Present tense Perfective/progressive aspect
1.	Kayode is doing the job.	Kayode has done the work	Kayode has been doing the job
2.	The bush is being cleared.	The bush has been cleared	The bush has been being cleared.
3.	Tola was doing the work.	Tola had done the work	Tola had been doing the work.
4.	The job was being done.	The job had been done.	The job had been being done.

THE FUTURE

The future is usually expressed in English by the use of auxiliary verb- "shall" and "will" and having recourse to some time adverbials such as "tomorrow", the day after tomorrow" 'tomorrow week', "today week" etc. Nevertheless, there is no form of the verb in English to indicate futurity, and thus, no future tense. In sentences such as:

"I will come"

"They shall go" do not indicate tense,

but simply manifest the future or futurity.

PRONOUNS

RELATIVE AND PERSONAL

Pronoun is used instead of a noun and so helps us to avoid repetition.

1) **RELATIVE PRONOUNS**: Much pronounced relative pronouns are noted with the use of <u>who, whom, whom, which</u> and <u>that</u>.

All these do not only take the place of a noun, but also join two parts of a sentence. For example:

Rev. Jude is the manager of the Niger Food Company.

Rev. Jude will give a lecture on balanced diet at the College auditorium next Wednesday.

It should be noted that, these two sentences can also be joined as follows:

Rev. Jude who is the manager of the Niger Food Company, will give a lecture on balanced diet at the College auditorium next Wednesday.

WHO, WHOM

Relative pronouns <u>who</u> and <u>whom</u> (or relate) to persons <u>which</u> refers to things; <u>that</u> may refer to persons or things, especially when defining a particular person or thing.

i) Where is the book <u>that</u> you promised to lend me?

ii) Is that the shop keeper <u>who</u> just arrived?

iii) This is the biscuit <u>which</u> is meant to be given for your birthday.

iv) Can you remember the name of the salesman <u>who</u> called?

v) This is the chicken <u>that</u> I promised to kill for the new yam festival.

In addition, <u>whom</u> is grammatically correct in the following sentence.

The lady <u>whom</u> I met at the bar is the sales girl.

It is now more usual and common to say: The lady <u>who</u> I met…

The accusative "WHOM" is used after a preposition (from, to, by, for, with etc):

i) The landlord <u>from whom</u> I rented the house.

ii) The caretaker <u>to whom</u> I paid.

Nevertheless, it is now acceptable in English to use a more informal construction, with the preposition moved further back in the sentence:

i) The landlord whom I rented the house <u>from.</u>

ii) The caretaker whom I paid <u>to.</u>

However, it is also acceptable, and certainly more usual, to leave out the relative pronoun altogether:

"The landlord I rented the house from"

WHOSE: Possessive pronoun <u>whose</u> help join two parts of a sentence where one part relates to owner or possession. For example:

(i) The middleman demanded for thirty per cent of the total profit.

(ii) The middleman will have to cut down his percentage.

The two sentences could be joined as follows:

The middleman <u>whose</u> demand was thirty per cent of the total profit; will have to cut down his percentage.

Examples:

(i) She (Third person singular nominative) saw you

(First person singular accusative)

(ii) They (third person plural nominative) said the books were theirs (third person plural genitive).

(iii) We (first person plural nominative) helped them (third person plural).

VITAL POINTS TO NOTE IN USAGE

(i) Do not confuse the possessive use of pronouns with the possessive adjectives (theirs, your, our, it's, her, his, and my).

(ii) Avoid the constant mistake of saying:

Between <u>you</u> and <u>I</u>. You rather must say: between <u>you</u> and <u>me</u> because the preposition "between" is followed by the accusative case.

(iii) However, it is correct to say: 'It was I' common usage allows us to say: <u>It was me.</u>

(iv) Never use an apostrophe with the genitive case.

Write theirs, not their's.

REFLEXIVE PRONOUNS

Reflexive pronouns reflect the subject of the sentence and they each contain the word 'self' e.g. myself, yourself, himself, itself, ourselves, themselves, and yourselves. These could be made use of in sentence like:

- (i) You don't have to blame yourself, after all people know you are innocent.
- (ii) Snake can bite itself.
- (iii) You knew, we got to pity ourselves.
- (iv) They themselves know the truth, that Jesus is our messiah.

Reflexive pronoun also can be used simply for emphasis: e.g. the doctor himself confirmed that the patient is a H.I.V. carrier. Note that in this sentence the writer draws attention to the important person (doctor) by adding 'himself' for emphasis. Nevertheless, it is worth knowing that is not proper to use a reflexive pronoun as a personal pronoun e.g.

Kemi and myself/himself traveled to Lagos yesterday (wrong)

The right form should be: Kemi and I/him traveled to Lagos yesterday (correct).

PERSONAL PRONOUNS

These words are: I, He, you, she, it, we and they. All these are referred to as personal pronouns. They are usually divided into these groups:

(a) First person pronoun: refers to the person or persons speaking: usually noted with the use of I, me, we, us, etc.

(b) Second person pronouns: refers to the person or persons spoken to: i.e. 'you'.

(c) Third person pronouns: refers to the person, persons, things or things spoken about with the use of He, Him, She, Her, It, They, Them etc.

It should be noted that, the forms which personal pronoun take depends on their use, such as being maybe i.e.

    (i) The <u>object</u> of a sentence (referred to as the <u>accusative</u> case.

    (ii) The subject of a sentence (referred to as the <u>nominative case).</u>

    (iii) Or indicating <u>ownership</u> (referred to as the genitive case).

SINGULAR	(OBJECT) NOMINATIVE	(SUBJECT) ACCUSATIVE	(OWERSHIP) POSSESSIVE OR GENITIVE
FIRST PERSON	I	Me	Mine
SECOND PERSON	You	You	Yours,
THIRD PERSON	He, she, it	Him, her, it	his, hers, its
PLURAL	NOMINATIVE	ACCUSATIVE	POSSESSIVE OR GENITIVE
FIRST PERSON	WE	US	OURS
SECOND PERSON	YOU	YOU	Yours truly,
THIRD PERSON	THEY	THEM	THEIRS

POSITION OF RELATIVE PRONOUNS

It should be noted that, a relative pronoun is expected to be placed close to the words to which they relate. For instance, take a look at this incorrect sentence.

The articles title on Nigeria's economic woes <u>which</u> will be published by the tribune next month. X should be written properly as:-

The articles which will be published by the tribune next month, was titled Nigeria's economic woes.

WHICH (special use}

At times we make use of the relative pronoun <u>which</u> in place of an action or complete statement, for instance:

(i) The president dish-out some relief packages, <u>which</u> made him very popular. (which here refers to the relief package).

(ii) Charles Taylor has broken the accord <u>which</u> put an end to any hope of peace in Liberia, (which here refers to the broken peace accord).

INTERROGATIVE PRONOUNS

Essentially used when <u>asking questions:</u> e.g. Who? What? Whom? Which, whose? It also has its nominative, accusative and genitive cases respectively.

and plural	Who What Which	Whom What Which	of what Whose of which

Examples are:-

(i) What is it?

(ii) What ate my apple?

(iii) Which among these is yours?

(iv) Whose Bible is this?

(v) To whom does the newspaper belongs?

(vi) Whose Koran is it?

DEMONSTRATIVE PRONOUNS

It functions just as its meaning. Demonstrative pronouns are depicted by the use of:-This, these, that, those etc to point-out or demonstrate a particular person or thing. It can also take the place of a noun:

It should be noted that one should not confuse a demonstrative pronoun with the demonstrative adjective, because the adjective is usually used with a noun, and never occur by itself e.g.

(i) These sailors are the captains of a ship – (demonstrative adjective used with the noun) sailors.

(ii) These are carnivores (demonstrative pronoun replacing a noun e.g. animal or man).

INDEFINITE PRONOUNS

This is used for nouns that have not been clearly defined or stated. Hence they do not stand for any definite noun.

Examples:-

(i) Every body agrees that they are going to vote for him.

(ii) All have sinned and shall repent.

(iii) When they were asked whether they are guilty or not, both men claimed the latter.

Also make sure you don't confuse the indefinite pronouns with the indefinite adjective. That is, if it is used to describe a noun (and not in place of a noun) then it is an adjective.

PUNCTUATIONS

These are the several marks used in writing and the commonest ones are:

1. **FULL STOP: (.)**

One thing to note about this mark is that, it is written as two words, not as one word or a compound word. (as some wrongly hyphenate them). A sentence however, has been said to be a group of words that begins with a capital letter and ends with a full-stop or a question mark or period. From this working definition, it can be seen that every non-interrogatory and non-exclamatory sentence <u>should</u> be terminated with a full stop! Which is the main function of a full stop (punctuation mark). It should however be noted that any sentence that is not rounded off with a full stop, should not be seen as a sentence at all.

Period or full stop is also used to abbreviate words e.g. Dr., Prof., Mr., P.M., A. M. Unicef. U.N.O., B.B.C. etc.

2. **THE COMMA** (,): This seems the most difficult of the punctuation marks as regards it's usage. Thus, a careful study of it's use should be noted. Example as follows:

USAGE:-

(i) To separate items in a series.

He brought home, his wives, children, servants, and dogs.

He came, saw, fought, and conquered.

(ii) To mark off words and expressions as in short; 'Nevertheless, 'However, 'for instance', 'therefore',

(iii) To mark off the addressee:

"Dr, your idea is ill-conceived" he retorted.

(iv) To show the beginning of a direct speech;

Boss said, "Driver, you are fired".

"Tell me Pastor" he asked "How hard is it for a Carmel to pass through the eye of a needle"?

3. **INVERTED COMMAS (OR QUOTATION MARKS) (" ") (' ')**

(i) Used to enclose words of direct speech. Usually double inverted commas are regarded as standard;

The single kind is used for a quote inside a quote e.g. I heard the policemen shout "Watch out, the ('criminal') has a gun".

(ii) Shakespeare said "Beauty is in the eye of the beholders".

4. **THE APOSTROPHE: (')**

USAGE

(i) To indicate possession;

(a) This is a man's world.

(b) Peter's daughter was kidnapped.

(c) Children's playground should be hitch-free.

(ii) To indicate a letter omitted: don't, shan't, it's (it is) won't, aren't etc.

(iii) For plural of letters and figures:

Dot your i's and cross your t's

5. THE DASH (-)

USES:-

(i) To enclose a parenthesis:

The liberty stadium – a symbol of Nigeria's love for soccer.

(ii) To show that a sentence was some how interrupted and therefore uncompleted: e.g.

(a) It is not that I hate you, but the truth must be told and the fault-

(b) Some body in the audience said "He knew where the secret –

6. THE QUESTION MARK: (?)

Used to indicate questions asked e.g.

(i) What is your name?

(ii) What time is it?

(iii) Why play truancy?

(iv) Can I light my cigarette, please?

7. **EXCLAMATION MARK (!)**

Used to indicate a surprise tone of voice after exclamation or vigorous commands.

    (i)   Oh My God!

    (ii)   Blimey!

    (iii)   Whao!

    (iv)   Watch out!

    (v)   Take cover!

It should be noted that just one exclamation mark (!) is necessary.

8. **CAPITAL LETTERS:**

Uses:

    (i)   At the beginning of a sentence.

    (ii)   At the beginning of a quotation

    (iii)   For proper nouns and proper adjective.

    (iv)   For all titles applied to one particular person.

           e.g. Nigeria is larger than Togo in terms of population.

9. **THE HYPHEN: (-)**

Uses

    (i)   In composite words: or compound words

          Sitting-room, drawing-room, thirty-four , ball-room game, double-standard, Black-board.

(ii) Used to indicate the completion of a word in another line, because it can't be done according to syllables:

e.g. essenti-ally

nevethe-less

writ-ing

read-ing etc.

10. **THE COLON: (:)**

Uses:

(i) To introduce a quotation

The actor said: "can't wait any longer".

(ii) To separate co-ordinate clauses when subsequent clauses explain, modify or explain the first.

GRAMMATICAL FUNCTION AND DESCRIPTION OF WORDS

To be able to treat this aspect of English very well, there is a great need for the English learner to have or acquire a detail study of the parts of speech as such be equipped with the "mechanics' of language.

Usually students preparing for the Senior Secondary School Certificate, and it's equivalents, normally finds it very tasking to delve into the complexities involved in noting the grammatical description or function of words or certain expressions, as may be given by the various examiners.

However, the below shown, guidelines and examples, stand to give them a good lead thus, serve as an eye-opener for them.

Example:

Fascinated by the gifts the Madam made to him, he immediately moved into her apartment in Ketu and lived with her until she abandoned him there.

    Fascinated: participle, qualifying the pronoun "Madam"

    By: preposition governing the noun "gifts"

    The: determiner specifying the noun "gifts"

    Madam: noun subject to the verb " made"

    Made: verb agreeing with the noun "Madam"

    To: preposition, governing the pronoun "him"

    Him: pronoun, object to the preposition "to"

    He: pronoun, subject of the verb "moved"

    Immediately: advert, modify the verb "moved"

    Moved: verb, agreeing with the pronoun "he"

    Into: preposition, governing the noun "apartment"

    Her: determiner, adjective possessive qualifying the noun "apartment"

    Apartment: noun, object to the preposition "into"

    In: preposition governing the noun "Ketu"

    Ketu: noun object of the preposition "in"

and: conjunction, co-ordinating the clauses "He immediately moved... apartment "and" He lived....her ... together

lived: verb, agreeing with the subject "He"

with: preposition, governing the pronoun "her"

until: conjunction, joining together the clauses "and (he) lives the her" and "he abandoned him there.

she: pronoun, subject of the verb "abandoned"

abandoned: verb, agreeing with the pronoun "she"

him: pronoun, object of the very "abandoned"

there: adverb, modifying the verb "abandoned"

DETERMINERS, PREDETERMINERS AND POST-DETERMINERS

DETERMINERS: These are words that mark the presence of nouns; In essence they announce the coming of a noun. Commonest determiners are the articles- the- referred to as <u>definite</u> e.g. The, A and the indefinite e.g. an etc, the possessive. Adjectives such as our, their, my and others such as each, another, enough, either, some etc.

PREDETERMINERS: These are words that preceeds determiners in a sentence one known as pre-determiners. Such words are <u>both, half</u> and <u>all,</u> e.g.

(i) Both girls are alike.

(ii) All of them are bloody drunkards.

POST-DETERMINERS: They follow determiners. These include numerals and ordinals, as well as 'very', 'few', 'many', 'less', 'most', same, other etc. e.g.

(i) <u>very</u> smart guys are rare these days.

(ii) The most essential commodity now is a jar of milk.

Note: The vital thing to note about determiners is that they are in complementary distribution; thus they do not trespass on each other's territory for instance 'my', 'this', 'can never' co-occur as in; this my car is very attractive.

ADVERBIAL PHRASES

A phrase is a group of words without subject or predicate. The grammatical functions of single-word adverb, some times can be performed by a phrase, this then could be called an "ADVERBIAL PHRASE".

EXAMPLES OF ADVERBIAL PHRASES

1. The Yorubas used to bring up their children <u>by traditional methods.</u>
2. Anthony stood <u>on the platform.</u>
3. The car leaves the park <u>at five O'clock.</u>

Like a single-word adverbs, adverbial phrases, too are broken into four types, they are:-

(i) Adverb of manner

(ii) Adverb of place

(iii) Adverb of time

(iv) Adverb of degree.

Examples:-

(a) A short while ago - adverbial phrase of time.

(b) with the utmost care - adverbial phrase of manner.

(c) Round the corner – adverbial phrase of place

(d) To a large extent – adverbial phrase of degree.

FORMS OF ADVERBIAL PHRASES

Special forms of adverbial phrases using prepositions abound such as at, on , in and can only be learned by use

e.g.

    at as in –at first

    at as in –at length

    at as in –at last

    at as in –at most

    at as in –at best etc.

ON

On as in on foot

On as in on time

On as in on principle

On as in on balance

On as in on purpose

IN

In as in vain

In as in force

In as in advance

In as in time

BY

By as in by surprise

By as in by service

By as in by accident

By as in by chance etc.

    It should be noted that all these are the various forms by which Adverbial phrase operates.

THE CLAUSE

A clause: - This is a group of words that forms part of a sentence and has a subject and a predicate. Hence, it is quite different from a phrase, which usually lacks both subject and predicate.

In a clause, we have a main clause and a subordinate clauses. A main clause can stand on it's own, since it expresses a complete thought. It is also referred to as an independent clause e.g. As Kaye lay on his bed that night, gazing at the ceiling, he thought over the matter"

Phrase here is:- gazing at the ceiling.

The clause is (a) As Kaye lay on his bed that night (sub-ordinate)

(b) He thought over the matter (main clause)

TYPES OF CLAUSE

1. **Adjectival Clause**: This performs the word of an adjective by describing a noun or pronoun in the main clause. It normally starts off with a relative pronoun, who, that, which, whom and whose.

EXAMPLES

The hunter who killed the lion lives on the mountain top.

At times the relative pronoun is skipped, out it's function is understood:

Who is Bola coming back to meet?

In the above statement the relative pronoun "who" is understood after "Bola".

2. **Adverbial Clause:** It performs the function of an adverb by telling us more about the verb in the main clause. Usually introduced by words such as when, where, although, after, as, because until, unless, while, before etc. e.g.

The wrestling match should have ended up in round ten <u>when the refree declared the winner as a result</u> of an unexpected knock-out.

Adverbial clauses are usually noted for that additional information to the main verb. They are as follows:-

(a) <u>Time, place and manner</u> e.g.

When Martha was in Germany he visited the home of Hitler (Adverb of time).

(b) **Purpose and Reason**

(i) The lawyer pleaded for leniency because he thought his client is guilty. (Reason).

(ii) The bouncer stayed at the entrance of the hall to ensure that everybody paid (Purpose)

(c) Concession: This used to depict a sub-ordinate clause which concedes a contrary point. It's usual introductory word is ALTHOUGH, e.g.

Although his father was very poor, he managed to acquire a great wealth through shear hardwork.

(d) Result: Words such as so and such followed later in the sentence by that expression a result, e.g.

The cost of foreign exchange now is so outrageous that people now make do with the onerous task of salvaging the American economy.

(e) Conditions: Words such as if and provided are used to express conditions e.g.

    (i) What will you do if you get home to find your apartment broken into by robbers.

    (ii) Obama might win a nobel peace prize provided he had averted the Russian war.

3. NOUN CLAUSE

This performs the function of a noun; e.g. How often the permanent secretary come to the office is nobody's funeral. It should be noted that the sub-ordinate clause in the above sentence has the function of noun and a subject of the sentence. Note that it is very essential that the sub-ordinate clause is placed as close as possible to the noun, verb, or adjective it qualifies, neglect of this can lead to lack of clarity.

FIGURES OF SPEECH

The idea of figures of speech is embeded in human language experience and expression, we can't dissociate ourselves from this natural reality, every language in the world has some measure of this writing devices, hence, it is in our language examinations, and this calls for the need to study them.

In this exercise we are going to treat the major ones or the commonest devices in writing, these are: simile, metaphor, irony, antithesis, hyperbole, euphemism etc. These are the commonest ones and this often appears in examinations on languages. Popular similes are often described as clichés-expressions which are over-used.

1. SIMILE:

This has to do with comparisons, usually introduced by the use of AS or LIKE e.g.

(i) His office is as dark as Satan's hell fire.

(ii) The ground was as flat as a table top.

(ii) He drinks like a fish, God save him.

(iv) He looks like a sickler.

2. **METAPHOR**

It is also a comparison between two things or people, but it does not use the words as and like. E.g.

(i) He is a lion – meaning he is very strong.

(ii) He has an iron will – strong will

(iii) She is the root of the trouble – she is the cause of the trouble.

(iv) He is the pillar of the family – he is the bread-winner of the family.

(v) She lives from hand to mouth – she is poor and manages to survive.

(vi) The ship of Greece's economy is heading slowly and definitely towards an iceberg. That is the nation's government will soon have problems (economic problems).

3. **IRONY**

This is the figure of speech employed when one wants to deliberately say the opposite of what is meant, but a way which lets the reader know the author's real meaning. That is saying of the opposite of what one intends e.g.

(i) The best way to pass your examination is not to attend lectures.

(ii) The best way you can drive better is by closing your eyes while driving.

(iii) The fire is so cold that he dropped it immediately.

In essence, irony is saying the opposite of what one intends,- highly deceptive.

4. **HYPERBOLE**: Is the use of exaggeration, which we are not meant to be believe, in order to create emphasis e.g.

    (i) He runs faster than a leopard.

    (ii) Heavens themselves blaze forth the death of princess.

    (iii) He is such a strong man that he is capable of lifting the whole building with just one hand.

5. ANTITHEIS:

This is the deliberate use of contradicting ideas, e.g.

    (i) Here today; gone tomorrow.

    (ii) Once beaten twice shy.

    (iii) Necessary evil.

    (iv) Speech is silver; silence golden.

6. **EUPHEMISM**: Saying of unpleasant things in a pleasant way e.g.

    (i) John kicked the bucket – John is dead.

    (ii) Attack is the best form of defence. (Attack first)

DIRECT AND INDIRECT SPEECH

Direct Speech: This form is employed when one writes the actual or exact words of the speaker. Forms of words like these are normally proceeded by a comma and inverted commas, to show that, that was how the words were really spoken out by the speaker.

Examples:-

(i) George Bush said "We shall attack the Iraqis unless they surrender".

(ii) Our principal said "Any student caught throwing papers on the floor will be given twelve strokes of the cane".

INDIRECT SPEECH: Another word for this is reported speech, it is a form that says or gives the words of the speaker as reported by someone else. Such reports are usually introduced by the use of a verb of <u>saying</u> in the past tense form.

This kind of expression is usually common among, the newspaper workers especially the journalists or reporters etc they always make use of indirect speech to express the ideas or speeches of public figures and important personalities during lectures or public speech.

Examples:

(i) The Governor vowed to put a stop to embezzlement of public funds in his State.

(ii) May told her sister to stop crying.

RULE GOVERNING THE SHIFT FROM DIRECT TO INDIRECT SPEECH.

(a) The words showing names in place and time becomes words showing distance or farness.

    (i) Today becomes that day

    (ii) This becomes that

    (iii) Yesterday becomes the day before

    (iv) Now becomes then.

(b) First and second persons pronouns (I, You, We) changes to the third persons pronoun, e.g. (He, She, They).

(c) Present tense becomes the past tense

    (i) Shall becomes should

    (ii) Are becomes were

    (iii) May becomes might

    (iv) Has becomes had.

(d) Clauses with the verb of _saying_ in the past tense sometimes indicates what kind of statement was made. Verbs such as urged, replied, ordered, declared, demanded, enquired, advised, suggested etc are often put into use.

Examples:

    (i) "Get me a good cane" said the principal (direct).

    (ii) The principal _urged_ him (student) to get him a good cane (indirect).

(iii) "What is your surname"? he asked the student (direct).

(iv) She ordered him out of his car (indirect.

SOME VERB YOU CAN USE APART FROM SAY

Distress, groan, cry

Command, dictate, direct, insist, order

Request, as, beg, entreat, plead, request

Agreement, agree, confirm, assent, admit Argument, protest, reason, state, urge, confess, argue Refusal, contradict, refute, deny, forbid

"SURE SUCCESS" ESSAYS & LETTER WRITING SKILLS

ENGLISH LANGUAGE

ESSAY WRITING

This will serve as a test of linguistic ability which will include, ability to write effectively, in a given situation.

Grammatical competence in areas of mechanics as well as an effective organization of the material is tested and credits are given for the following.

(a) Adequate arrangement of material (logical sequence)

(b) Appropriate paragraphing

(c) Use of formal or informal features where appropriate

(d) Appropriate use of Dictions

(e) Mechanical accuracy (punctuations/spellings).

(f) Adherence to the given rules and regulations i.e. time allowed, length, expected, etc (400 words).

LETTER WRITINGS

TYPES OF LETTER WRITINGS

1. Formal letters
2. Informal letters

- **Formal letters:** This is a form of letter writing meant for strictly official purposes; e.g. a letter to a Newspaper editor, school principal;, business letters, application letters etc. It is strictly formal in forms and culture, and the mode of discourse is usually formal and straightforward. In writing a formal letter, one must eschew the flow of sentiments, unruly and impertinent use of language.

FORMATS OF A FORMAL LETTER

```
                                    YOUR ADDRESS
                                    ……………………………..
                                    ……………………………….
                                    ……………………………….
                                    Date
```

```
ADDRESS OF YOUR ADDRESSEE
i.e. WHOM YOU ARE WRITING TO
```

Dear Sir/Ma,

TITLE OF YOUR LETTER

* START HERE

INFORMAL LETTER:- This is a form of letter written to someone to who you are very close with e.g. letter to one's parents, brothers, sisters, uncles, friends, pen-pals, cousins etc. It should be noted that any letter that falls in the above category is essentially informal, in form and outlook. Sentiments and emotions could be brought to bear depending on closeness.

FORMATS OF AN INFORMAL LETTER

```
                                    YOUR ADDRESS
                                    ……………………………..
                                    ……………………………….
                                    ……………………………….
                                    Date
                                    i.e. 23rd May, 2015.
```

GREETINGS

Dear Thompson,

Or

My Dearest Uncle,

GUIDELINES

    (i)   Introduction – Exchange of pleasantries

    (ii)   Body – your main points

    (iii)   Conclusion – summary of main points.

SUBCRIPTION

i.e.

your loving brother,

Knowles

or

Best wishes

Katie

Informal letter contd.

NOTE:-

1.   You should realize the importance of organization, that is you must arrange address properly putting the relevant punctuations – it is essential for you to note that your full stop ends with the final word and the date i.e. 23rd June, 2015.

EXAMPLES

1)	Croydon Prescent Road	ii)	40 Oxford Street
	CR0 10EZ		Mushin,
	Croydon.		Lagos
	23rd July, 2015		2nd July, 2015

1. Note where the comma and full stops are placed and that there is a little space or gap between Lagos and the date.

2. Note the need for paragraphing- that is, your ideas must be in paragraphs, thus making your work neat and easily readable.

3. Note the importance of indentation and paragraphing, continue your letter, beginning each new paragraph directly under the place where your first paragraph began.

4. Also note the need and uses of capital letters where necessary e.g. for proper nouns i.e. names of people, towns and cities.

5. Put the appropriate punctuations where required, since this helps the reader to comprehend the ideas you are trying to put across.

6. After you might have finished your writings or letter you put your subscription – this is your submission, e.g. for informal letter.

(i)	Yours loving son	(ii)	Yours affectionately
	Thompson		Trevor.

TYPES OF LETTERS AND RELATIONSHIPS

We have 3 types of letter writings namely:-

(i) Formal letter – official letters written to an organization, school principal, club letter.

(ii) Informal letter- to relations or family e.g. to father/mother, friends etc.

(iii) Semi formal letters e.g. letters between a working colleagues.

However, it should be equally noted that, there exist some relationships between the writer and his addressee. These relationships are:

(i) Formal relationship (ii) informal relationship

(ii) Semi formal relationship

i. FORMAL RELATIONSHIP: Under it we have:-

(a) Tutorial relationship, e.g. teacher/student relationship.

(b) Job relationship e.g. worker/manager relationship

(c) Business relationship customer/Bank manager/staff

(d) Public relationship e.g. citizen/Governor/President relationship.

ii) INFORMAL RELATIONSHIP

(a) Family relationship e.g. Son/Father/Mother/Uncle/Aunty relationship.

(b) Friendly relationship e.g. Friend/Friends relationship or Pen friend/Pen friend relationship.

iii) SEMI-FORMAL RELATIONSHIP

    (a) Acquaintance Relationship e.g. student/pen friend.

    (b) Group relationship e.g. club members/association relationship/worker and colleagues relationship.

LETTER WRITING

A letter writing could be seen as a composition. It is a continuous writing and it is addressed to some persons, this part make it a little different from an essay per se.

It should be noted that a letter has seven parts:

    (i) Writer's address and date.

    (ii) The addressee's name or official title and address.

    (iii) Opening courtesy

    (iv) The caption or heading of the letter.

    (v) The content or message (body of the letter)

    (vi) Well-wishing or gratitude

    (vii) Closing courtesy or conclusion.

1. ADDRESS OF THE WRITER AND DATE:- This is usually written at the right top corner of your plain sheet.

EXAMPLES AS FOLLOWS:-

> Oyo State School of Nursing,
> P.O.B. 90
> Ibadan,
> Oyo State,
> Nigeria.
>
> 6th May, 2015

Note: It should be noted here that this part contains six items among them are the name of the institution, postal number, state, country and date. A very important point to note is that, there is a comma (,) after every item and that the final one is marked off with a full stop (.). also note that the date is separate a little bit from the whole item and marked off with a comma and a full stop. It is noteworthy that each item stands on separate line.

2. **THE ADDRESSEE'S NAME (OR OFFICIAL TITLE) AND ADDRESS**

It is noteworthy for the writer, to realize that the persons to who the letter is been addressed to is referred to as the addressee.

Practically, all formal or official letters contains the addressee's name or official title. The addressee's address is usually written on the top left corner of the page starting on the line below the line on which the date is written.

Example:

> The Commissioner,
> Ministry of Works and Housing,
> Awka,
> Casablanca.

3. **OPENING COURTESY**: The function of the opening courtesy is to politely invite the attention of the addressee to the content of the letter which will follows. Opening courtesy is usually written below the addressee's address and well separated from it, moreover, the space between the margin of the paper and the opening courtesy should be same as that between the margin and the items in the addressee's address. It is also noteworthy, that the opening courtesy should be marked off with a comma (,). Nevertheless, various forms of letter required various forms of opening courtesy e.g. Dear Sir, or Dear Ma.

4. **HEADING/CAPTION**: This simply means, the topic about which the letter is to be written. All formal or official letters are bound to have such heading or captions.

Example: **'APPLICATION FOR THE POST OF A LECTURER ASSISTANT'.**

Note: (i) That a caption is written on a line below that on which the opening courtesy is written.

(ii) Words in the heading are usually written in capital letters.

(iv) Underline the whole heading as above.

The importance of the heading is to let the addressee or reader of the letter know what the letter is about before reading the whole content.

5. <u>CONTENT OF THE LETTER</u>: This is the real message being delivered to the reader. This par has three parts namely:

(i) The introduction

(ii) The body

(iii) And the conclusion

It follows this pattern, because whenever we are writing a letter, we have some ideas or information to communicate to the addressee, the ideas are initially introduced in the first or earlier paragraphs, we will proceed to give details of those ideas in the body paragraphs; and will conclude the ideas in the last paragraph. These occur only on the details of the content only, of the letter.

6. WELL WISHING: After finishing with the content of a letter, it is necessary therefore to note that there is a great need to thank the reader for reading your letter or for whatever he/she has done for you in the past or for what you expected him to do for you.

Examples:

(i) Thanks a lot

(ii) Thanks for anticipated co-operation.

(iii) Thank you Sir.

(iv) Bye for now.

It should be noted that, well-wishing or gratitude is expressed immediately after the concluding part of the content section and that the expression begins on a fresh line and is indented, just as a new paragraph.

7. CLOSING COURTESY: This consists of the identification of the writer and the form of relationship existing between him (writer) and the addressee (reader), the signature of the writer and his name is written down at the extreme right hand corner of the bottom of the letter.

(i) For a formal letter, you use the following closing courtesy:-

      Yours faithfully,

      (Signature)

      KemiKazim.

(ii) For informal letter it is:

      Yours affectionately,

      Funmi. Or

      Your loving son

      Tawa.

PRACTICE THESE EXERCISE ON YOUR OWN

1. Tell an experience that depicts the maxim.

    "Not all that glitters are gold".

2. Write your own contributions to your school debate

    Arguing for or against the topic "Why we needed a woman president than a man in China's Polity".

3. Write an official report to be forwarded to the police, district officer, reporting the constant menace of armed robbers in your living area or street, advising on how they could be put to check.

4. Write a letter to your school Principal, requesting him to help ameliorate the standard of sanitation in your school, acquainting him with the deplorable state of school's sanitary facilities. Suggest to him how best he can restore them.

5. An article has just appeared, in one of the national newspapers, on the topic "Why for students unrest"- write to the editor, your own contributions and suggest a better way of handling such issues and that you wish it published.

QUESTIONS

ESSAY & LETTER WRITINGS

QUESTION 1: You have been invited by a youth organization to speak on 'Indiscipline among youths'; write out your speech.

ANSWER: Good day, Mr. Chairman, Lady Chairman, my Fellow Youths, Ladies and Gentlemen. It affords me a great joy and opportunity to air my views on the reason for wide spread of indiscipline among our youths, in recent times.

To start with, what is indiscipline? According to Chambers Dictionary, it defines it as a want of discipline that is total deviation, from decorum and moral etiquette.

This is what our youths indulge in these days, thus the subject matter calls for an urgent public and government attention, so as to rescue our posterity from the dangers inherent in these forms of deviation, that metamorphosis into outright indiscipline.

To tackle this issue, one first need to address the causes of indiscipline.

The causes are as follows:

First and foremost, we should realize that during the process of a child's biological march from early childhood through adolescent to adulthood, he must have undergone various societal influences and changes with which he wishes to arm himself or herself for the societal task ahead. Thus, the negativity or positivity of this societal influence, is to a large extent determined by the natural environment in the society, in which the child grew up.

Another cause of indiscipline, could be through the child's peer group in schools, if he keeps the company of smokers, drugs addicts, robbers etc he is definitely bound to involved himself in these activities.

Moreover, the advent of civilization also aids indiscipline among our youths, a typical example could be seen in the way they total submit to the ideas and actions they witness in the various western films they watch. They tend to act and dress like the protagonist of any film they have watched and enjoyed.

These examples are manifested in the general out look of our youth, they no longer observe the normal rule of dressing, the females among them will want to put on the most outrageous hair cut and outfits that tend to make them look half naked. All theses are done in the name of fashion. This total disregard to positive culture, is gradually eating deep into the fabric of our societal sanity.

Furthermore, the present socio-economic problems of our nation also add a feather to the cap of indiscipline in our society.

This is also manifested, in a situation whereby the lucky wealthy few, daily oppress the poor without a care in the world.

The result of this is that, the desperate few undertake various forms of crime, as a survival mechanism, their criminal activities ranges from murder; robbery to drug trafficking, and what is the consequence on our country? All over the world an average youth of today is believed to be a drug trafficker and a dupe- that is obtaining under a false pretence as a way of life.

After all said and done, we should not allow these ugly situation to haunt us forever, thus, we need to devise a modus operandi with which to demystify this myth of indiscipline.

And the steps are as follows: First and foremost, there is need for a mass education programme, that is, a certain governmental organ should be responsible for educating the masses on how to observe discipline and moral etiquette by doing a honest work and living a honest life, that is, life devoid of immoralities, such as theft, embezzlements and other crimes to mention a few.

Another step is the need for the parents to expose their children to honest living and dignified life, by watching them closely and correcting them each time they seem to deviate from what ought to be. The reasons for parental intervention at this juncture is very important because most adolescents lives are tailored to their parents or guardians' life styles and tastes, because the children sees the adults as their role model and thus emulate whatever they (adult) do, regardless of it's (actions) moral stand and consequences.

Finally, the society and the government need to compromise on what is expected to be the acceptable moral standard in our societies and thus mark out praises and damnation. The former for a person who is honest and hard working in the society, while the latter should be for the likes people with questionable livelihood.

And to crown it all the government should promulgate certain laws to deal accordingly with the law breakers and moral decadents in our society.

Dr. A D GabrieAsutech

QUESTION 2: Write a letter to the newly-elected Chairman of your local government council congratulating him on his election and stating the priority needs of the people of your community.

ANSWER:-

Obosi Grammar School,
P.O.Box 121,
Uruowulu,
Obosi

25th August, 2016

The Chairman,
Obosi Local Government Area
Obosi.

Dear Sir,

Priorities of Obosi Community.

This letter is intended as a medium of congratulating you on your success, in the last chairmanship election, in which you won with a majority vote under the platform of S.D.P., once again, accept my congratulations and I wish you a happy tenure in office.

As we are all aware of the fact that, Obosi community is a community beset with a multi various problems, in which one finds it tasking, to point out, the areas due to be given a priority, having in mind, the evirons geographical location, historical importance, agricultural viability among other things.

Since we are aware of the fact that resources are scarce these days, hence it is imperative to point out the viable and pressing needs of the people and thus making those needs our priority.

As a result of this, I suggest that our priorities should include these aspects and projects, namely, the provision of pipe-borne water, provision of electricity and finally the repairs of our roads, throughout the local government areas, most especially, the roads that leads to the various farm settlements.

Now, to expatiate on the reasons for these postulations, to start with, the need for adequate provision of pipe borne water. It is a common knowledge that, various communities in Obosi lacked adequate supply of pipe-borne water, hence majority of the inhabitants often take solace in making do with the available streams and rainfall, which is usually occasional and seasonal.

When rain stops, the people usually face extreme hardship, some will have to trek up to ten to fifteen kilometers before they could get a drinkable water. Last year, the entire Obosi community witnessed a serious worm epidemic in which many lost their lives as a result of inadequate financial stand to cater for a proper medical treatment. We now think it's high time, something is done to avoid further epidemics, since we all know that prevention is better than cure, this is why the issue of the provision of adequate pipe-borne water required no further delay.

We have rivers surrounding us which could be damed or possibly embark on sinking of bore-holes in communities, if the former idea seems to expensive.

Secondly, the provision of constant electricity supply also should be made a priority. It should be noted that, practically nothing could be achieved, administratively, industrially, economically and commercially without adequate supply of electricity; this matter calls for urgent attention because all the machineries that help to carry out or accomplish the productive functions in the above named fields, wholly depended on the uses of adequate power supply for effective functioning and that is why it (power supply) should be made a priority, since the future of our community really depended on their viability, (of these industries).

Finally, the issues of good and motorable roads, should also be seen as a priority, this is borne out of the fact that, without the provision of good road, that allows for a free flow of traffic, it will be extremely difficult to carry out any plausible transportation activities, like taking a lorry to and from farm settlement; in order to transport some newly harvested agricultural products, to neighboring towns and villages, this activities, the members of the community who are predominantly farmers, found extremely difficult, and even when they succeed in getting a vehicle for this kind of job, the cost and expenses they bear is usually alarming, and when they eventually bring those goods to the community markets, their prices are usually outrageous because they have already included costs of their earlier expenses on transportation and labour. However, regrettably those (farmers) who cannot afford the transport cost for this kind of operation, usually leave most of their harvested agricultural products to rot away in their various farms, after which they might have taken the quantity that will suffice them and their immediate family.

The point to address now, is that the local government should endeavour to repair most of our bad roads, fill the pot-holes, since the cost of tarred road is now too expensive to embark upon, it is advisable to device an alternative means of repairing the bad ones (roads) and extend them to the various farm settlements to allow for easy transportation within the local government areas and her neighboring environs.

Sir if these advice are taken seriously, it will go along way to ease the problems of your administration and on the other hand earn your government a worthwhile reputation and acceptance by the populace, thus possibly prepare you for a second term in office.

Yours faithfully,
Kola Obosi.

QUESTION 3: You have just spent your holiday in another part of the country with a friend. Narrate your experience to other friends, describing what you found interesting about the customs, foods, dress and way of life of your hosts.

My Stay in Uruowulu-Obosi

One man's meat, as they say is truly another man's poison.

This what I realized when I stayed at Obosi in Idemili local government area of Anambra State with my friend Uju Osakwe.

The first thing that struck me about the Ibo way of life is their kola-breaking tradition. The Ibo people believe so much in breaking kola and they do so at any gathering or when they have visitors. They use the kola to pray for protection and guidance from God after which the kola is broken into small pieces and passed round to the people present.

Another aspect of their way of life which also interested me was their way of greeting people. Unlike the Yoruba people who believe in kneeling and prostrating (female and male respectively) for their elders, the Igbo people do not believe in such. Rather, they shake hands no matter how older the other person is. Another thing connected with this, is showing appreciation, once the Igbo man has thanked you for whatever favour you granted at that time you granted it, he believes that is all. This of course is different from the Yoruba practice of thanking you at every opportunity after the favour. This is so because the Yoruba believe that if you do some body a favour and that person does not thank you the day after that means he can never get anything from you ever again.

Concerning food, the main food of the average Ibo man is cassava and its various products like 'Akpu', Garri, and 'Abacha' which I jokingly tagged rice because it is grated into spaghetti-like strands. One interesting thing about the eating habits is that they hardly put oil in their soups and stews because they believe eating too much oil especially palm oil gives you malaria-fever. To the Igbo man no soup is worth its salt if you don't add vegetables to it and the funny thing is that things Yoruba people believe to be weeds are regarded as indispensable and nutritious vegetables.

Igbo people, both male and female dress in a striking and beautiful manner. The women's outfit normally consists of a blouse, two wrappers and a head-tie. Men's outfit is somehow similar in that men also dress in a shirt, a wrapper under the shirt (as opposed to the women who tie their own wrappers over the blouse) and a cap. This cap is either red, if the man is a titled man or any colour if he man is common man.

Igbo people have their own distinctive customs of burial, naming and marriage ceremony. Immediately a man dies, most especially if he was a tilted man, cannon-shots called 'Egbenduru' would start booming from morning till night up to the burial day. On the burial day, there would be feasting with a lot of drumming and dancing before and after the man is buried. On the following day, masquerades will come out as a form of honour to the dead man. One aspect of the Ibo custom of burial which is more baffling than interesting is the eating and drinking that takes place when a young man of around 20-30 year is being buried. I curiously asked some Igbo people the reason for this and they could not give a convincing answer other than it is what they've been used to. There is no specific custom in the case of naming a child, people name their children before or after birth. Unlike the Yoruba who name their children on the 1st day or months after birth.

In the case of marriage; if a young man finds the girl of his choice, he, together with some friends and elders from his family will go with the girl to her parents to inform them of the man's intention to marry their daughter. The parents will tell them that they should come back at a certain time after which they must have asked their daughter if she is ready to give her consent. When the girl has signified her own consent the parents will send for the man and his people to negotiate with them and they will inform the man that he has to take the girl out for shopping to buy certain stipulated things for her. After this, the girl will follow the man home to stay for a week, this custom is called 'Imala-ani' (knowing the land). This is to enable the girl judge whether she can live with him or not, if the girl says she cannot live with him after that week, the parent will tell the man not to go ahead with the traditional wedding. To the Igbo, this traditional wedding is a good enough marriage and it only depends on the couple to have a church or civil (court) marriage.

All in all I had a nice time inObosi because the people are very hospitable. If I had waited long enough I would have witnessed the New Yam Festival which I was told is also very interesting to experience. The festival normally involves the whole community and is celebrated in merriment and feasting because of the belief that the earth god has blessed them with the new yam and so he must be praised- Miss Nike Ogunbiyi.

QUESTION 4: A friend of yours has been absent from school for about a month due to illness. Write a letter to the friend describing some interesting things that have happened in the school during the period and expressing your wish for a quick recovery.

Pacific Correspondence,
P.O.Box 2112,
Colorado,
USA.

Dear Tunde,

It is very unfortunate that your protracted illness that we thought is not going to last long; is taking you a month now. May God give you the required energy to recover soon.

Anyway, I considered this letter useless if I failed to inform you about some interesting things that have happed in the school for the past one month. As you know that it is was barely a week to our 'Literary and Debate Week' that your illness started, it was quite sad that you are not around. Your class teacher expressed openly, how much your absence was seriously felt. Those two boys that represented your class could not perform up to expectation, your class came last.

Last week Friday marked our principal's forty years on earth, it was fun throughout. We were surprised that our principal knew so many important people, the Oba was there, the State Governor and the Senior Executive members of he House. Our school was painted red, it was taken by storm.

No student could claim of not been fully fed that day. The band stand was the renown Police Band. Those people can play! It was that day that I truly believed that Kings do not dance at parties, the Oba just sat watching throughout the event. The day's activities were rounded up by our schools Dramatic Society and the Cultural Group. That Seyi, I hope you could remember her- the cultural group leader; made up to one thousand dollars that day. She was highly commended for her beautiful dance steps and the sonorous voice.

Conclusively, I will like to bring to your notice that the school is planning seriously towards the opening of our new Administrative Block. You know the building has not been deckened by the time you last came to school, I really hope you will recover soon to come and witness how beautifully completed the building is. Not only the colour of the paint used in painting the building but also the beautiful flowers that were contracted to a renowned horticulturalist. They are beautifully arranged.

I wish you soonest recovery.

Yours sincerely,

Segun Banjo.

QUESTION 5: Write an article, for publication in a national newspaper, on the dangers of drug among youths.

DANGERS OF DRUG USE AMONG YOUTHS

Permit me a space in your widely read newspaper; to air my views on the dangers inherent in drug addiction among youths.

There is no fire that burns without smokes, that gives credence to the fact that, a child does not just grow up in a day and start taking drugs, hence there should be a casual factor. By this, one means that something or someone introduced the youth into this ungainful exercise of drug addiction.

The reasons below could be advanced and seen as an eye opener into what brings them (youths) into drugs.

First and foremost, the peer group influence, this is determined by the type of school and the company of people the youth keeps, if the majority of his or her group are drug addict, definitely the unwary innocent youth, could be overtly or covertly involved in this clandestine exercise of drug addiction.

Other factors that lead the youths into drug is lack of family/parental care, in a situation whereby the parents are often away and not have such time to spend in the major role of child's upbringing, then the youth (their children) takes freedom for license, thus indulge in all kinds of drug addiction and possibly into drug pushing. Because of the parental neglect of acquainting themselves with their children's companions or peer groups and the kind of influence, the members of such group might inculcate into the young minds of their neglected children are often overlooked by such parents.

Moreover, most youths are usually shy, when out in the public. Most especially, when they make up their mind to act tough on their parents, teachers or friends, they discover that they can't just naturally be tough except under certain influence, to them, the answer is usually drug addiction. Under this influence, they normally succeed in accomplishing any tough acts they intend to embark upon gradually it becomes a permanent habit for them, to the extent that they at times mix with dubious persons. In a wider society, people with questionable livelihood are usually associated with drug abuse and trafficking, possibly during one of the youth's occasional visit to the drug peddler's depot, he may meet with these dubious personalities, who could introduce him/her into a fast money-making-gimmick of drug trafficking, and finally gets the youth ruined. When luck runs out on him during one of his consignments.

Now, to address the question, on the dangers inherent in drug addiction, it should be noted that drugs generally are noted to have side effects what more, it's addiction! The dangers ranges from general misconduct to total mental illness. How do these come become? One may ask. The fact is that, the youth whose mental capacity is weak may not be able to withstand the tasking and overbearing pressures of powerful drugs like cocaine, heroine on his brain. Thus, in the process his/her situation may get out of hand then he ends up with a severe mental breakdown; thus becoming a societal nuisance and a total disgrace to his entire family.

Drug addiction aids immoralities, like sexual abuse, rape, armed robbery, smuggling, criminal activities and other innumerable social vices , and immoral acts. Since these drugs could help by encouraging their underworld activities by giving them (culprits) the undue courage, effontry and rationale, thus urge them on to committing these unwholesome acts, or which the consequences are usually borne by the innocent members of the society who are upright and law abiding.

Furthermore, a close study of the youth drug addiction goes a long way show the deplorable state of moral decadence in our society.

The youths no longer listens to his or her parents and easily gets annoyed irritable and destructive on slight provocation when on drugs but after the drug's effect on him wears down, we then looks so gentle and remorseful, after which he must have destroyed invaluable items or properties.

In conclusion, a close study of the above-mentioned points clearly shows that, to eradicate this issue of drug abuse/addiction, the society and government has a great role to play.

First, the government must show her contempt for drug trafficking and drug peddling by detailing some special squared to apprehend them, and bring them to book.

Again, the government should also organize a mass literacy campaign to educate the masses on the evil of drug abuse through mass media houses via both visual and audio-visual means.

Lastly, the society should co-operate with the government by forming some vigilance groups within communities, who will report any drug peddler or user to the Police for apprehension.

The last but not the least, the society should endeavour to change heir believe of placing high premium on personalities with ill-gotten wealth and thus praise and reward shear hard work and honesty in it's stead.

- Dele Emmanuel
Washington DC

QUESTION 6: As the Senior Prefect in your school, write out the speech you would give on the occasion of your school's end-of-year ceremony. Mention some of the problems you faced and give suggestions on how they could be solved.

END OF THE YEAR CEREMONY

Good day Mr. Principal, Vice Principal, members of the Staff, Fellow Students, Ladies and Gentlemen. It affords me a great pleasure in delivering this speech for today's end of the year ceremony in this our great citadel of learning.

I greatly thank the principal and other members of the staff for bestowing me with this great honour of becoming the school's Senior Prefect, this gesture is really appreciated and on this, I promised to live up to expectation and never to indulge in anything that may bring disrepute to my great school. It's been six months now, since I've been handling this mantle of leadership, and of course, it will be an understatement if I should say that there hasn't been any difficulties, in my way towards dispatching of my duties. As well as I knew well of the fact that, uneasy lies the head that wears the crown, nevertheless, I strongly believed that I'm equal to this onerous task and daggers drawn in the bid to tackle these problems.

Among the problems faced is that of discipline, we are also all aware of the fact that, the notorious cancer worms of indiscipline has shamelessly eaten deep into the fabric of our moral discipline and etiquette. It should be noted by all and sundry, that this deplorable moral standard can no longer be tolerated in this noble school of ours. One may want to ask what discipline is he talking about? Then I stand the chance of putting it to every one here that, these act of indiscipline, dominating our moral standard ranges from lateness to school to total disregard and disobedience to staff and prefects alike. This show of shame must be stopped hence forth, if we all will have to live together like brothers and sisters and not like the proverbial cats and dogs.

Another serious problem one use to face in this school is also the problem of maintaining a reasonable hygiene standard, students are fond of throwing around dirt and scraps of used papers and litters all over the school premises, I seize this opportunity to implore my fellow students to observe the rules of hygiene, and also noting the fact that it is not just the sole duty of the health or labours prefect alone to see to the neatness and general cleaning of the school, we should all stand to gain good health from observing the rules of hygiene, on this premises I wish to advise my fellow students to please check and correct the culprits among us.

The last but not the lest, is the problem of inadequate power supply and pipe-borne water supply which the students always complain to me about, several times. I've appealed to the the school authority on this issue and obviously nothing tangible has been done to ameliorate this deplorable situation. However, I also seize this opportunity to plead again on behalf of the entire students of this noble institution the school authority to please do something concrete and attend properly to this issue that demands urgency.

In conclusion, all the highlighted problems are what I've been experiencing since I 've taken up the mantle of leadership as a senior prefect of this school, and I hope for a change for the better next session when we resume, to note critically, the highlighted problems of indiscipline, hygiene, pipe borne water supply and inadequate power supply, that have been our lots in this school, hence device a modus operandi with which to solve these problems come next session.

Thanks,

Damian Kings

Senior Prefect.

COMPREHENSION PASSAGE

WHAT THE. EXAMINERS EXPECTS FROM YOU

This section will consist of two prose passages between 250 – 300 words long. The question that will be set on these passages will test the candidate's ability to: -

(a) Find appropriate equivalents for selected words and phrases.

(b) Understand the factual contents that are categorically stated;

(c) Make derivations and inferences from the content of the passage.

(d) Respond to uses of English expressions to reveal/reflect sentiments/emotions/attitudes;

(e) Identify and label basic grammatical functions of individual words, phrases or clauses as they appear in the content.

(f) Recast phrases or sentences into grammatical alternatives.

The passage will be written in good contemporary prose that will be within the scope of the candidate.

Q.7 READ THE FOLLOWING PASSAGE CAREFULLY AND THEN ANSWER THE QUESTION WHICH FOLLOW: -

Though Hitler is dead, many mysteries about him remain unraveled, especially the mystery of how he was able to rise to supreme power. The source of his strength, the nature of his ultimate beliefs, and the workings of his fatal weakness, all these would be debated for many years to come.

No final assessment could be made at the time, nor can we reasonably expect to reach a final assessment in our generation. Hitler's <u>verdict</u> on himself was given in the testament he drew up the day before his suicide. It was an <u>astonishing</u> and revealing document. Having sacrificed millions of Germans to his own glory, he claimed that all his actions had proceeded out of love and loyalty to his people. With perfect <u>detachment</u> and single-mindedness he claimed that he had shown the German people the way which destiny had pointed out to them, and it was not his fault that they had proved unworthy of the task. He urged the Germans to continue the struggle. While he was <u>dictating these words,</u> the Russians had encircled Berlin and the chancellery was being bombarded by Russian guns at close range. Hitler wrote that he chose to die by his own hand rather than <u>submit</u> to cowardly abdication or capitulation. But the most revealing paragraph of his testament referred to his possession, which he <u>bequeathed</u> to the party, or if the party was no longer in existence to the state should the state too be destroyed, no further decision on my part is necessary.

(a) From the passage, what type of ruler was Hitler during his life?

(b) (i) How did Hitler die?

(ii) Why?

(c) What was the last thing Hitler did before his death?

(d) At the time of his death, how was Germany performing in the war?

(e) What two options did Hitler give for disposing of his possessions?

(f) For each of the following words, find another word or phrase that means the same and which can replace it in the passage.

(i) Mystery

(ii) Verdict

(iii) Astonishing

(iv) Detachment

(v) Submit

(vi) Bequeathed

(g) "While he was dictating these words"

    (i) What is the grammatical term used to describe the above expression, as used in the passage.

    (ii) What is the function of the expression in the sentence?

        a. Hitler is a dictator, he rules by dictatorship.

        b. (i) He died by his own hand, committing suicide.

            (ii) Because he doesn't want to submit to the cowardly capitulation of the Russians army.

        c. He bequeathed his possessions to the party or stat in absence of the former or to none if the state becomes destroyed in the cause of the war.

d. Germany had already lost the war to the Russians.

e. He drew up a testament urging the Germans though having failed to accomplish the path destiny has chosen for them, should not lose hope but continue the struggle.

f.
   i. Mystery – wonder
   ii. verdict – pronouncement
   iii. astonishing – surprising
   iv. detachment – determination
   v. submit- yield
   vi. bequeathed – willed

g.
   i. conjunction 'while'
   ii. the conjunction 'while' helps to co-ordinate or serve as a link between the earlier expression "…to continue the struggle" and "while he was dictating…" thus stating the adverbial time of action.

ESSAY AND LETTER WRITING

Question 1: Your school was tipped to win the final match of the <u>inter-school football competition</u> for secondary schools in your state, but unfortunately <u>you lost to the underdog.</u> Write an article for publication in your school magazine on that match, explaining <u>why your school lost</u> and lessons to be learnt.

In writing this kind of essay or article, it is imperative that you should note the basic ideas to be tackled in the question as the underlined above. After this, try as much as possible to map out an outline stating your guidelines and points in a logical and sequential order, gradually allowing the ideas to flow freely into one another. This will make your article to be very interesting and worth reading.

Q 1: ANSWER:

e.g   <u>Why we lost the state inter-house secondary schools football competition</u>

The last state inter-house secondary schools football competition, which our school activity participated in to the extent that we entered for the semi-final and won, thus warming up for the final match, for which our various fans and admirers have already tipped us to win. Since they have reposed so much confidence in us, we should have lived up to their expectation by winning the glorious cup, but as fate would have it, we (our football team) came, crashing down like an ill-fated airbus.

However, one should not see our failure to excel in the competition as a complete soccer disaster or as a failure story, but rather see it in the terms of the old proverbial saying that "When a young man falls down, he stand up to continue his journey, but when an old man falls, he looks back to know the cause of his fall and note it" in the light of this situation, we the entire students of this college should see ourselves as the latter, that is the old in the above adage.

This is to say that, our failure should rather be seen as in eye opener rather than a morale burster. Since we should all realize that mistakes are said to be the beginning of experience and experience the beginning of wisdom so let it be to us.

I could quite recollect the fateful day when our gallant players- "the great conquerors" stormed the field Ogbe stadium in Edo State. For this much talked about football competition, we all had it at the back of our mind that we are going to win our opponent – "the great lions".

Immediately the match commenced, our boys undoubtedly began to perform very well, especially during the first half of the match, though there was no goals on either side but, our players- player numbers 10 and 2 had already sustained some injuries on their right and left ankles respectively, and immediately the whistle went off to mark the end of the first half time. I reported this to our games master, showing him the players who sustained the injuries, he (games master) dismissed by argument that they should be replaced, claiming that they are one of his best players, and that he cannot afford to replace them with those in the reserve list, who are tested to be equally good.

Also, I noted that the boots which our players were using are of the inferior quality and some had already torn, and the players were merely managing them, while their jerseys are of different colours, this of all things, I first detected, since it is quite difficult for our players to easily identify themselves, on the field hence countless times, they mistakenly passed the ball to their opponents out of confusion, even some of our players were wearing a blue jersey, which happens to be the very colour of the jersey which our opponents wore on that fateful day.

All these I had pointed out before the second half, but when I wouldn't say that all these solely led to our purported ill-luck in the competition but at least it adds to it or probably the god of soccer had suddenly stumbled on an idea, and decided to punish us by leaving our camp for the camp of our opponents- "the great lions".

Nevertheless, to be candid with ourselves, it is quite obvious that the school authority merely wanted us to do the job, neat and fine, but declined to give us competent tools for its final accomplishment- these ideas of sub-standard boots and jerseys readily points to this.

In addition, I suggest that our players should be subjected to marathon exercises and football practices so as to always be in form for the greater task ahead, all I'm convinced of is that those cups belong to us, we shall win them, when the time is ripe, we'll march forward to claim them, we must not lose hope and patience, because they (cups) rightly belong to us and next competition will prove us right.

Kenneth

Labour Prefect.

Q.2 Narrate a story to illustrate the warning:

"Look before you leap".

ANSWER:

This topic reminds me of a particular incident that occurred during my early school days in the City College, Lagos. This school is noted for the lackadaisical and non-compromising attitudes of her students, which range from truancy among the newly admitted students to their seniors in the final classes.

It all happened that there were some group of girls in the final classes, who simply will not care a hoot whenever any teacher or even the principal tries to call them to order.

The activities of these young girls or does one call them ladies are dubious, in the sense that, you never can tell wherever you could meet them at a point in time, because they are all over night clubs and cinemas like a locusts for multitude, though some of them are from a well to do homes, but I believe that the bitter fact, is that most of their parents prefer their multi-various businesses to taking good care of their children, today they are in the country, tomorrow they are in overseas on business trips.

Among these girls is a single one named Toyin, she happens to be the group leader or does one call her the groups pacesetter, she single handedly monitors and decides the lines of action that they will take at any point in time. Their activities ranges from going out with the very wealth young men in town to the keeping of very wealthy elderly men tagged (sugar daddies) whose source of enormous income are tantalizing but questionable.

Days turn into months and months in years, keeping up this kind of a life style, they all passed out of the school but with a result the could scare an examiner. They had to stay at home and re-enrol for another final school examination, with events taking over things, I happen to know Toyin very well because she lives in the same estate as I do, but her friends are scattered all over the country, some even traveled out to overseas to seek greener pastures.

The last straw that broke the camel's back was when Toyin had to dump her year long boy friend, who is an accounting student at the University of Lagos for very wealthy young man living at Allen Avenue in Ikeja, Lagos, this young man has series of flashy sport cars, I guess with this, he totally blind folded Toyin, but Toyin never bothered to inquire about the sources of this young man's vast fortune, rather she proposed to him and already carrying his five months pregnancy, they decided to get married.

To the greatest shock of every one on the very eve of their wedding, this young man was whisked away by the Interpol with the aid of the Nigerian Police Force, for allegedly being a most wanted drug baron and an international dupe. It was reported that his latest drug consignment was a total flop and led to his arrest as one of his agents confessed under a severe torture by the American Police.

The last report that we heard about the young millionaire was that he has been sentenced to a fifteen years jail term in America. Had Toyin "looked before she leaped she would have averted this kind of ignominy and disgrace ".

QUESTION 3: There have been wide spread compliant by students against the teaching staff: absenteeism, lateness to class, failure to prepare lessons, and so on. As the senior Prefect, write a letter to the Principal, informing him of the situation and requesting him to take necessary action in order to avert a riot that is being secretly planned by students.

Oduduwa College,

P.O.Box 168,
Ile-Ife,
Osun State
2nd June, 2016

The Principal,

Oduduwa College,

Ele-Efe,

Dear Sir,

Complaint of students against the teaching staff in our school.

This affords me a great opportunity to acquainted you with the general situation of our school's activities, and more importantly to notify you of the impending chaos and disaster that is imminent and surely will come to be, if a drastic and a positive approach towards correcting it, is not brought to bear.

It has now come to limelight and the generality of the students now openly complain about the laxities inherent in the members of the teaching staff in our school.

These much talked about laxities among them ranges from lateness to school, total absenteeism, failure to prepare the lesson promptly, among others.

Sir, it is now an open secret that all students have vowed to embark on a rampage if this obnoxious act of indiscipline should persist, and names had already been marked out for attack, the ball is now in the court of the authority to map out a nice strategy with which to handle this- sitting on key of –a-gun power-like situation, I further advise that no act of vindication will be tolerated neither victimization nor any undue expulsion will be entertained the reason being that even the parent/teachers association are well aware of this terrible ordeal we students are facing presently, and they are now waiting patiently to see the school authority's reaction before they finally carry out their decision, this is why this situation requires a cautious and proper handling if normalcy is expected in due course.

Furthermore, the negative effect of this ugly situation if it's not immediately taken care of, will be likened to a three-pronged fork attack, firstly, on the school authority, the students and lastly the erring teaching staff.

In fact if this situation should linger further, these three parties will surely have a tale of woes to tell, the school will lose her long acquired and jealously guarded reputation, the students will fill the streets causing general pandemonium and untold havoc while the entire teaching staff could lose their jobs- this is why it is imperative to act now!

Yours sincerely,

Kingsley O.

Senior Prefect.

QUESTION 4: The Political Science students' Association in one of the higher institution learning has invited your school to participate in a debate on the topic: "Civil rule is preferable to Military rule".

Write out your speech for organist the motion.

ANSWER:

"Civil rule is preferable to Military rule".

Good-day, Mr. Chairman, Lady Chairman, panel of judges, co-debaters, my fellow students, ladies and gentlemen

It affords me a great pleasure and privilege to be here today, to state my views against the reasons for Military rule, rather I would be happier to prefer civil rule over a military rule in view of the reasons below:

First and foremost, what is a military rule? More so, what is supposed to be the function of the military? Is it the act of governance or warfare? The answer is obviously the latter.

All over the world it is noted that the function of the army is to shield the nation's territorial integrity against any external or internal attack, thus their wild idea of eyeing the nation's most exalt presidential post on is simply borne out of greed disloyalty avarice and sheer indiscipline. This act is usually seen as a deliberate attempt in undermining the nation's integrity, little wonder, they indulge in gross abuse of the presidential office- show a former Nigerian Military leader who is not a multimillionaire now, as soon as they become the head of state through a bloody coup de tat, their next port of call automatically becomes the Swiss bank, there they siphon our hard-earned currency and what is the result now- we now wallow in economic quagmire, and now design an awful feeding formula of 0.1.0 meals, our once buoyant economy, has now become a shadow of its past self.

Secondly, we should not forget that nobody every voted the military to power, they came there neither through the people's mandate nor through democracy but through a coup de-tat, in which possibly there was a blood bath of the innocent citizens. A government which is not of the people's mandate is not supposed to be in power, I rather see the military in power as traitors who have betrayed their fatherland by turning against the much cherished democracy, which we all have vowed to uphold in principle and practice, what more, the mindless violation of their oath of allegiance as sworn on their first day in the force.

Thirdly, to bring home my points, I concede to my opponent's assertion that military has a way of enforcing their rules and regulations on the populace, but I will want to bring to light the issue of who has been longest; the military or the civilian regime?

Undoubtedly, the military has been the longest ruler in Nigeria polity and thus the most subversive. Their forces of coercion are negative and devoid of decency and moral principles, because of the way they just enact decrees that gives no regard whatever to human rights, not to talk of safety, and to crown it all, having being the longest in power, who then should be blamed for the nation's present economic predicament, focusing our outrageous debt increment. Obviously, the military should take the blame, because they have failed us in both principle and practice a situation whereby a whole military leader should be bold enough to tell his subjects on a national broadcast that the nation's economy (of Nigeria) has defied all possible logic, yet he still clings to power, for what? He wants to witness cannibalism among his subjects before he shamefully resigns.

Furthermore, I opt for a democratic government whereby the mandate of the people is well respected, civilian rule allows for an adequate exercise of human rights and privileges, devoid of unusual harassment and detention of innocent citizens simply because they point out the faults in a military regime. The military should be more enlightened so that they could be able to distinguish between the function of the military parse and politics. These happen to be two different things and poles apart, unless they transform under the dubious canopy of greed through a coup de tat to the nation's presidential palace, with their usually ignominious claim of coming to rehabilitate the economy which according to them, has being ruined by the ousted civilian regime-this broadcast with its attendants martial song is usually a shameful spectacle to behold.

Moreover, had the military allowed the civilian government and democracy to prevail, Nigeria would have been a better place for all by now.

The better fact that everyone must realize is that we are still a developing country thus still has a long journey ahead of us, and this is the more reason why the civilian regime should be given a chance to prove itself and bring the principles and practices of democracy to bear. If the military could stop their thief-in-the-night kind of pranks in our nation's political system, we will be better for it.

It is note worthy that in democracy, the electorates are well represented in both the senate and House of representatives, in which the nation's decisions are jointly made, unlike in the case of the military where some half-baked intellectuals under the guise of Armed Forces Ruling Council (A.F.R.C.) seats to decide the fate of our much cherished nation, in this kind of representation obviously there is bound to be biases since, it's only the minority that is being represented.

In conclusion, in the light of the above mentioned reasons, you will agree with me that a situation whereby decisions is reached by the general consensus of the people is better than in situation whereby just few men seats to decide on a nation's fate and whose decision is the final with the aid of some obnoxious monster they call the decrees, that has for our law courts of the land

Thanks.

QUESTION 5: You change school recently and have been at the new school for six weeks, write a letter to your uncle explaining why you left your former school and describe at least three things you find more interesting in the new school.

Ikare Grammar School,
P.O.Box 168,
Ikare
Ondo State.

24th May, 2013

Dear Uncle,

How is work, health and other members of the family? I hope they are doing fine.

This letter is meant to serve as a mine of information notifying you that, it is now exactly six weeks I've left my former school (Ibadan Boys High School) to the above named school.

Uncle, I really benefited by taking to the advice which you gave to me, the last time I came to spend my holidays with you in Jos, in which you mentioned the importance of making science subjects my priority rather than keeping to only arts subjects. This vital advise, I later found to be worth-while, because, when I discussed with my elder brother, who is now in his final year at the University of Ibadan, (studying Electrical Electronics) requesting him to advise me on what subject/s to choose for my SSCE examination, I was so surprised that he said exactly what you told me that day- that science courses are now the thing in the fast changing socio-economic, cum technological world of today.

Uncle, as you are aware of the fact that my former school, only offers arts and commercial subjects, and I as a person, have already made up my mind to study medicine in any reputable university in the country, hence I found the reason for my change of school worth the while, since my new school has an adequately equipped science laboratory with competent science teachers.

Secondly, it delights my mind to see that my new school has a standard social amenities for recreation, such as a large football field, table tennis equipments, lawn tennis courts, volley ball court, a fair sized swimming pool and some equipments for gymnastics to mention a few, nevertheless, it is worth while also to note that subjects class time-table, thus allowing us to make a better use of these numerable recreational facilities. Only very few of the afore-mentioned facilities existed in my former school.

Lastly, as you must have known that my new school (Ikare Grammar School) is a notable citadel of excellence, the school has produced numerous prominent sons and daughters of Ikare up to date, and its still relentless as you should know that it's always good for one to be associated with things of excellence and not mediocre, our teachers here, are worth their salts ad they are competent and dedicated to duty unlike in my former school whereby some of the female students were usually harassed by some teachers. At this juncture, it is important to notify you that my new school has enough hostel accommodation for boarding students, and hostel life makes one more discipline, academically and socially.

In conclusion, with the above explanation, you will now believe with me that by last heeding to your advice, I have made the right choice, sir, one day I will want to you come down to my new school to pay me a visit, then you will realize that seeing is believing.

Looking forward to receiving your reply soon.

Your affectionately

George

QUESTION 6: You were an eye-witness to a fire outbreak which completely destroyed the main market in your town. Write an article suitable for publication in a national newspaper describing the incident and suggesting measures that could be adopted to prevent a recurrence.

IHIALA MAIN MARKET FIRE OUTBREAK

Spare me a space in your Concord Newspapers to air my views as an eye-witness, on the recent Ihiala Main Market Fire Outbreak and moreover, to make my own suggestions as to how further likely occurrence could be put into permanent check.

It all started on the 12th of June, 1992. In the evening time, around 9.30pm on that fateful day, nobody ever anticipated such an outbreak not to talk of the cruel and wanton destruction of lives and properties by the fire.

Earlier on the total electric supply of the whole of Ihiala district was cut off due to the repeated heavy down pour and it's attendant storms that destroyed some electric poles, thus making it difficult for electric current to flow freely. Consequently, as a result of the unbearable total darkness which the entire districts were plunged into, coupled with the break down in production and other commercial activities in various indigenous industries, protests started coming up from various prominent quarters as to why the NEPA officials have delayed for so long in repairing the faults and thus bringing back the light for the populace and the various industries which are losing fast in their ventures as a result of this power cut-off.

At last, there were promises from the office of the National Electrical Power Authority (that is the district branch) that they are bent on restoring the electric light soon, and they gave a date to commence the repairs, this instructing people to switch off their electrical appliances and metres. So, the date was fixed for 12th June 1992. For the repairs and restoration of the electrical lights, as fate would have it, most people who were market men and women, whose trade in one way or the other has something to do with the use of electricity, were very happy and waited at their various stores patiently for the magic hours.

To everybody's surprise, nothing happened throughout the day time, and as soon it was 6.00pm to 7.00pm people began to lose hope feeling that they have been cajoled and hood winked by the NEPA officials, so as it was getting dark people began to return to their various homes, the fact being that the main market is quite far, just at the outskirts of the town and immediately it starts getting dark, there is every possibility that you may have to trek the long distance home, since no commercial vehicle will want to play the roads in the night for the fear of being a victim of the incessant armed robbers menace, which has been out of the police's glare for months now, despite the people's complaints.

At last, the right time came, it was around 9.30pm when the electric light came on, all over, people were shouting hey! Had most of them know, they would have kept mute, for ironically, that day came out to be the most awful day for traders whose shops and stores were affected in the main market. Because, immediately the light came on, fire burst out in some shops that had their meters and switch on, possibly the owners of such shops forgot to switch off their switches, thus fire burst out enormously destroying most shops, houses and properties worth millions, the few guards around that night, thought it was a child's playing until the situation really got out of hand. The official's reports from the government's investigators confirmed the fact that the fire outbreak occurred out of the negligence of some shop owners in putting off their meters and switches before leaving for their various homes.

Well the deed was done already but the future re-occurrence is what ought to be prevented now, in the light of this, I suggest that every trader should posses a fire extinguisher of various types, to help put off possible future fire outbreak in time, furthermore, the fire service brigade should endeavor to have a branch of their office nearby the main market with adequate fire equipment and vehicles, this suggestion is borne out of the fact that, this is the third fire incidence in this same market, this year alone, thus it calls for a real government attention.

Finally, people should be educated on safety, and precaution how to avoid fire outbreak and how to putt-off the already blazing fire, this could be advertised on mass media programmers' and should be government sponsored. Also, I advise or rather suggest that the government should make available various fire extinguishing mechanisms for sale at a highly subsidized rate, this will go a long way to sustain the nation's good, services and citizenry.

King Osodi

Lagos.

QUESTION 1: The Nigerian Orientation Movement has invited entries from final year Senior School students for an essay competition on the topic: "Corruption in the society: causes, manifestation and solutions".

Write your entry.

Corruption in the society

To start with, what is corruption? According to an advanced learner's dictionary, corruption simply means any form of abuse of office, illegal immoral demand and acceptance, which is contrary to the laid down official ethics or moral decorum.

Now the causes of corruption in our society could not be far-fetched as many socio-economic factors militate against the societal moral ethics and values.

First and foremost, the inability of a low-income earner to meet his/her financial demand gives room to all temptations thus morality is jettisoned and corruption becomes the order of the day.

Indiscipline, among others, is the root of corruption in all style and forms it may take, for instance, as a result of indiscipline, greed avarice, borrowed lifestyle, etc. becomes the order of the day hence the crime rate is always on the increase. Another is the emergence of the criminal code 419; surfaces as a result of corruption, many government officials threw official ethics and honesty to swine thus engaging in all forms of criminal activities, in order to satisfy their insatiable needs and greed.

The last but not the least, is the societal craze for wealth, not minding it's source, as long as he spends the naira, the society sees him as the most respectable and honorable. Societal premium on ill-gotten wealth ought to be checked lest danger is imminent.

After all said and done, we should realize that our (society's) blind love for money and corruption, has made us (Nigerians) an outcast in the international circle, other nations believed that an average Nigerian is a potential dupe and a cheat who trusts should not be bestowed upon. There is an unfortunate incident, and it has gone a long way to embarrass even the innocent and honest Nigerian, who happen to have traveled overseas.

Another manifestation of our corrupt lifestyle could be noted in the fashion craze of Nigerian youths nowadays, everybody wants to look like an American at all cost, not minding whose ox is gored or who gets dumped in the process.

Corruption has gone a long way to destabilize our economy and rendered our currencies impotent in the world market.

Nonetheless, the corrupt mind of our young girls has curried their love and chase for sugar daddies, not minding what comes out of such a relationship, as long as naira is made the watch-word.

After highlighting all these forms of corruption in our society presently, it is equally worth-while to proffer solutions.

First and foremost, the society needs to inculcate the spirit of discipline and hard-work; they should be made to understand that honesty is a virtue. Mass education bureau should be set-up to enlighten the masse on the need to inculcate moral ethnics and fairness in dealing with people.

The society should stop placing undue premium on people with ill-gotten wealth but rather scorn them.

Parents and government have a major role to play in societal cleansing, thus help wipe-out corruption in our society. This they do by re-orientating our youths (parents) while the government should enact laws to fight against corruption, only through these can Nigerian will ever gain back her lost reputation and credibility in inter-national circle.

Kingsley O.

QUESTION 6: You are participant in a seminar organized by the Directorate for Women Affairs on the topic:

"The Role of the Woman in Nation Building".

Write your presentation

THE ROLE OF WOMEN IN NATION BUILDING

Good day, Lady Chairman, Organizers, Ladies and Gentlemen, here present.

It affords me a great pleasure, to put across my views by highlighting once again, the roles Women need to play in the nation building.

These roles could be well stated by first trying to better understand what the parable "charity begins at home" entails.

It should however, be clearly noted that women (mothers) in attempt to create a better nation are squarely faced with the various problems that emanate from, home (domestic problem society and the nation at large, however on these premises a woman must strive to better the lots of the nation and her youths by contributing meaningfully, her quota, and the followings are how they go about it.

First and foremost, women (mothers) happen to be the first companion of the child hence should be expected to have a great influence on the child's life, thus she is expected to indoctrinate and inculcate, the desired social values, norms and ethics of the contemporary time, thus making the child to easily fit in properly in the society. One may tend to ask how the women go about to bring these desired influence on the child.

Then the clear answer to this it that, it's only the mother (women) who is so close to the child, thus knows all his or her problems, and possible solutions. The mother knows how to get her son or daughter to perform some domestic chores, instill discipline and the spirit of keeping the proper rules of hygiene in the child. The mother goes about all these by first wining the child over to herself, by showing him or her true motherly love and care.

In essence, this squarely points to the fact that the mother (women) is the major initial source of the child's socialization.

On the society, the woman, tries as much as possible to uphold moral principles and discipline, by example. She should try to always condemn the social ills and be able to speak the truth always without fear or favour, these go along way to help build a better nation.

Women, has a role of integrating and socializing various factions of the people in the society by preaching the need for harmonious co-existence among neighbors and family members by teaching them to show true love and understanding to themselves. All these help in no small way to enhancing nation building.

The last but not the least, the women also has a great role to play in the entire nation building by preaching and showing the spirit of true patriotism, by organizing seminars, workshops and conferences to discuss about vital societal issues to help create a better nation.

Women also play the role of a guidance and counsellor to children and adults in the society depending on their (women) intellectual exposure and life' experiences.

In conclusion, there is no gain saying that the role of women in nation building cannot be over looked, since there are totally indispensable to the normal development of the youths, society and nation in general.

WRITING OF A MINUTE OF A MEETING

1. (I) supposing you are the secretary of a club or any other organization and that you are therefore expected to write the minutes of the meetings of that club or social organization.

Then you should bear it in mind that, the task before you is that, the minutes you write are a summary of the discussion that takes place a particular meeting.

The issues to be discussed in such meeting are referred to as the "AGENDA FOR THE MEETING". Showing that the issues have been known and that under each issue, there will be some points, which will be made during the meeting. It is these points that you write the minutes on, note as you listen to the discussions, you gather the main or major points or ideas. As you listen to the discussion however, mention must be made of the name of any contributor of idea during the meeting and his or her ideas mentioned thereafter.

(ii) Lets say that, under the discussions the issue of "punishment for a member that errs or violates a certain laid down rules of the club" is under discussion, for example, many points may be made about it during the discussion. Note that, they're going to be several suggestions by members hence you will have to mention the name of any one that makes any suggestion, what he/she suggested and his/her reasons for the suggestion and the views of the house (all members of the club) about his/her suggestion, all these should be well noted.

At the end of various suggestions, there could be a vote to determine the stand to take by the (club members) this is usually determined through votes. Then after the general voting, any stand taken by the whole house is as the result of the majority vote stays. This decision should be noted in the minute as a very vital point by the minute writer or secretary of the club. All forms of writing these should be in the summary since, the writer cannot be able to write down everything that is said during the meeting.

(iii) After the minutes have been written, now the document differences. For instance:

    (a) A heading of the minutes will be written instead of a topic e.g.

    "Minutes of the meeting of Panther's Club, held at the palace hall on the 10th of June, 1992".

    (b) Preliminaries such as, saying the opening prayer, roll-calls of members present and absent are noted,

- the time the meeting commenced
- reading of previous minutes

- correction and adoption of minutes
- Matters arising from the past minutes.
- General contributions of individuals.

Furthermore, it should be noted, that each of these preliminaries is conducted briefly and briefly summarized by the writer of the minutes.

2. Issues discussed on the agenda will be summarized one after another in a logical and sequential arrangement to allow for easy reading and understanding.

3. The last issue usually raised is that of "ADJOURNMENT" the writer summarizes the "MOTION" and support for adjournment indicating their movers; i.e. "Mr. Dele Sana moved for the adjournment of the meeting" supported by Mr. Dada Ojo. The writer should state the closing time of the meeting as agreed by the house (club members). There is usually the need to serially number the items in the minutes as discussed, to allow for easy reference.

Finally, the signatures of both the secretary and the chairman at the end of the meeting are required for formality sake.

Q.8 READ THE FOLLOWING PASSAGE CAREFULLY AND THEN ANSWERS THE QUESTIONS ON IT.

When neighbors learnt that the Umorus' household had been raided by robbers, they were genuine downcast because the easy-going Umorus minded their own business and had contributed immensely to the development of the area. Visitors early that morning were shocked at the way the door were vandalized before the robbers forced their way into living-room to make away with the radio, the television, the wall clock, and the video cassette recorder.

As some sympathizers discussed the perfection with which modern robbers strike nowadays, a few of them drove to the police station and soon arrived with detectives. Quickly, statements were obtained from the couple and a few neighbors, all an attempt to pin down suspects.

From these statements, it was learnt that the bushes and uncompleted houses nearby had not been searched. The officer ordered his men to comb the bushes and the unfinished structures. While this lasted, he stood over the culvert near one of the buildings.

Thoroughly, form room to room, from tree to tree, the searchers toiled. But it was a fruitless exercise. The help rendered by neighbors did not yield clues. At last, the police boss concluded that the robbers were beyond their reach, and so called of their chase. He blew his whistle and ordered his men into the jeep. Reassuring Mr. Umorus that the search would continue, he instructed the driver to move.

All the while, in the culvert, their booty by their side, the two robbers snored on. Had a stray dog not given them away, later in the afternoon, they would have escaped with their booty.

a. Why were the neighbors concerned about the robbery in the house of the Umorus?

b. Identify the two types of synthesizers mentioned in the passage.

c. (i) Were the police careful enough in their search?

　(ii) Who do you think so?"

d. What finally happened to the robbers?

e. 'Had a stray dog not given them away'?

　(i) What is the grammatical term used to describe the above expression, as used in the passage.

　(ii) What is its function?

f. Give one word that could replace each of the following as used in the passage.

　I. Immediately

　ii. Vandalized

　　iii. Pin-down

　　iv. Comb

　　v. Structure

　　v. Chase

a. The neighbors were down casted because the Umorus are easy going and usually mind their own business; more so, they help to develop their community.

b. I. Umorus' neighbors

ii. Visitors early that morning.

c. I. No

ii. Because they did not search in the culvert and that we even stood there while the searching was been made by his men.

d. They were later betrayed by a stray dog while they were busy snoring. "Had a stray dog not given them away"

e. i. Adjectival clause (stray dog)

ii. It functions as a describer of the noun dog.

f. Greatly

i. Destroy

ii. Capture

iv. Search diligently

v. Pursuits

SUMMARY WRITING

QUESTION 9.   You are advised to spend about 40 minutes on this section.

A study conducted in Nigeria recently recognized three varieties of spoken English. Speakers of the first variety exhibit characteristics of a very long and difficult process of 'internal interpretation' from the mother tongue into English. Thinking and expression do not go closely together. A listener would notice this from the way the speaker pauses before expressing himself, apparently deciding which words to use and how to arrange them.

Thus, thinking is exclusively through the medium of the mother tongue and English is thus a poor shadow of the original thoughts of the speaker. Moreover, when discussing with other speakers, utterances heard invariably have to be translated silently into the mother tongue to be maximally meaningful, and then response are translated from the mother-tongue into English. Consequently, the long, indirect routes make statements slow, halting and jerky.

The second variety speakers exhibit features described above but to a much lesser degree. Internal translations from the mother tongue to English still take place during the speaker's expression of opinion and complex concepts but the process now takes a short span of time. With ordinary words or simple ideas, internal interpretations need not intervene between it is given verbal expression. Discussions are quicker and smoother though might not always entirely from minor halting gaps.

With the third variety speakers, thought is at most entirely in English and translation is not needed. The speaker has a wealth of linguistic weapon to choose from the express the minute distinction between similar concepts- and these come quickly and easily. Thus, for instance, whereas speakers of variety III recognizes distinction between "shower", "downpour", 'drizzle', 'mist', 'deluge', etc and uses each in the appropriate context. Also, his mastery of the sounds and features of the English language equips him express the utterances accurately and automatically without having to pause and think of the correct version of a sound since he masters the various distinctions in the pronunciation of each vowel and each consonant. We need to recognize, however, that most Nigeria learners of English 'graduate' from one variety to another, from the lowest stratum of variety 1 to the highest stratum of that variety, and then to variety II and so on until they achieve variety III. Length of periods of education, exposure to standard English and a personal speaker uses. Finally, we must recognize the most speakers of the higher varieties are still capable of reverting to the lower ones, if they choose. Thus we can find even a Nigerian Professor or phonology switching to.

SUMMARY

A summary is merely the rewriting of passage or idea expressed in a long sentences into a contracted meaningful precise form. That is the breakup of a long explanation or sentences into few meaningful lines without loosing the credibility of the original message and content.

A SUMMARY PASSAGE

CASE AGAINST CONSPICUOUS CONSUMPTION

Conspicuous consumption is one of the major reasons why our dear nation lost the golden opportunity provided by the oil boom of 1973-1983. it led to the oil wealth being spent on importation of luxurious cars, foods, trinkets, and clothing, when it could have been used in embarking on self-propelling growth.

It made us looks with disdain on our local foods and handicrafts. How many of our people today are not ashamed of taking bread fruit and palm kernel, wrapped beans, and palm wine, while proudly taking Champaign, cream of mush room soup and spaghetti? Are we not thereby supporting the overseas farmer while discouraging our own farmers?

Yet every day, developed countries keep teaching us lessons. When the price of oil increased, the white man reduced its' use, developed domestic sources of it, and substitutes for it, and so forced the price down. But when the prices of foreign goods increase, the craze for them increased in Nigeria and they are even declared essential commodities. We queue for hours for them. Rather than seeing offences as crimes against society, offences are now viewed by individuals through heavy lenses of selfish, professional, clannish and sectional interests.

This brings about one of the biggest contradiction of social inter-relationships in contemporary Igbo land by which people tend to apply double-standards in judging their own conduct of others. As a result, it is now becoming true that vicious acts become vices only when they are committed by others, but virtues when committed by ourselves or our relations. For instance, the official who embezzles public funds, and sets up a chain of houses all over the place is corrupt if he is an outsider, but clever and dynamic if he is myself or my brother.

A student who cheats in his examination should be expelled if a stranger, but recognized as fast if he is my son. The trader who short-changes, adulterates, and exploits, a rogue if a stranger, but is doing "biz" if my brother. In a nutshell, these have been our lots, we bask under the cloak of oil boom-oil shall go one day, we all know this and then we will learn to bask in oil-boom, after we might have met our waterloo-then and only then we shall learn lets pay God it's not too late.

TACKLE THE FOLLOWING SUMMARY QUESTIONS

1. According to the author, what in a nutshell causes our economic woes? Give two clear examples as cited by the author.

2. How did the white-man according to the author use to 'teach us lessons"?

3. In a single word what did the author claimed to have brought the "biggest contradiction".

Read this passage carefully and answer the following questions-

1. Choose a word or phrase to replace the following words:

   (i) Conspicuous

   (ii) Befitting

   (iii) Investing

   (iv) Practices

   (v) Public Health Institution

   (vi) Dismay

   (vii) Canonizing vice

   (viii) Research that has long gestation period

   (ix) Out of tune

   (x) At its heights.

2. in two sentences list, what the author feels that has contributed to our economic woes.

3. What is the grammatical function of:

   (i) "Public health institution"

   (ii) How does it function in the passage

4. Explain in you own words what the author means by the use of "conspicuous consumption" not in more than 3 lines.

5. What did the author suggest that we should have been doing instead of diverting our working to leisure? Write in not more than 3 lines.

Conspicuous consumption is out of tune with the economic realities of today. Obviously in the later seventies and very early eighties when the economy was at its height, people made easy money- on Federal Government Contracts, in smuggling, importing and exporting, clearing and forwarding etc.

So it sounded meaningless asking people not to spend lavishly, money they made to easily. Those days money was indeed out the problem but how to spend it. The word "billion naira" crept into out daily vocabulary. (Called from the address of Pita No Ejiofor- Anambra State Commissioner for Finance and Economic Planning 1986) on crusade against squandermania.

COMPREHENSION PASSAGE

FOR PRIVATE PRACTICES

Conspicuous consumption diverts our resources from working to leisure and from investment to consumption.

Many a time offices and markets are closed to give the dead a so-called befitting burial. The time we spend in long wake-keeping ceremonies, numerous marriage ceremonies like bachelor's eve, house warming ceremonies, second burials is spent by the white man in his library or laboratory researching on how to develop the machinery he will later export to us. The money we spend on those occasions is spent by him in taking a balanced diet and investing in shares and stocks.

Some of these practices are now terribly costly to our society. For instance, the woman whom tradition requires to sit for one month inside the room as a mourner may be a surgeon who should be saving lives in one of our public health institutions.

She may be a college principal who should be maintaining discipline in her school. New wine has been put into old containers. One of the major causes of frustration and the so-called bad attitude to work of our workers who watch with dismay the society's canonizing vice, celebrating ill-gotten wealth and forwarding money made today by all means instead of hard work, and investment in research that has long gestation period.

SUMMARY

a.(i) In Latin America students are reported to have sold their shoes to pay for classes in English speaking teaching programme.

(ii) A tribal Chief of Africa was once turned away from enrolling due to lack of adequate chair, but the following day he reported again with his contingent carrying their chairs with them.

(iii) It is noted that today in U.S.A. there are greater numbers of students now than there was forty years ago.

(iv) The United States Information Services Libraries in the third world enjoy academic facilities yearly and the Soviet Union also dispatches enormous number of books in aids for the developing countries of the world.

b.(i) The writer postulates that education has now graduated from a mere luxury to a necessity in order to meet the now complex industrialized society.

(iii) That formerly jobs are usually filled for people with adequate strength and native intelligence but now jobs call for a possession of a college degree.

SUMMARY PASSAGE

QUESTION 9:

Read the following passage carefully and answer the question on it.

On a global basis, no statistics are adequate to suggest the magnitude of the revolution in education today. In the United States Information Services libraries in the third world, about thirty million people annually use the facilities provided. The agency distributes over one hundred and fifty every year. The Soviet Union also distributes over one hundred and fifty million books to developing countries all over the world. But together, these programmes do not come near to meeting the world demand.

Mere facts and figures cannot convey the human passion for learning. In the English –speaking teaching programmes mounted for children in Latin-America countries, children have been known to have sold the shoes off their feet to pay their way to classes. In Africa, a tribal chief was turned away from enrolling in a class because there were no more chairs. The next day, he and a contingent of his fellow chiefs were waiting outside the door, each carrying his own chair.

This revolution is not limited to the developing world. In the United States there are more than fifty million student more than 185,000 public and private schools at all levels. There are more students today in the United States than there were city residents only forty years. We have entered an age in which education is not just luxury, which gives some men an advantage over others. It has become a necessity without which a person is defenseless in this complex industrialized society. Levels of education which were once regarded with awe have now become commonplace. And jobs which once could filled with possession of strength and native intelligence now call for a college degree. We have truly entered the century of the educated man.

It is a mistake however, to confuse skill with education. A man who has been taught only to hold a job has not been educated; he has only been trained. And the man who has merely been trained is not fully qualified to take his place in a free society as a fully participating citizen. An all-round education should equip the learner for any challenges he may encounter.

Education, of course, is not something that is acquired just in college. It is a life-long task and when I think of death, I think of it as the moment when the brain ceases to inquires and expand.

(a) In four sentences, one for each, summarize the instance given by the writer to show that education is speeding at a very rapid rate.

(b) In two sentences, one for each, state the reasons given by the writer to support the view that education changing fast.

SECTION 1: COMPREHENSION PASSAGE

Answer all the questions in this part. You are advised to spend 45 minutes on this section.

Q.7 Read the following passage carefully and answer the questions on it.

Do the present policies on those who commit crimes reflect a lass war? For long, people have alleged that certain laws discriminate against some members of the society while such laws favor others. Besides, some sociologists also claim that some members of the society are more prone to some specific crimes than others. So, our opening question if <u>pertinent</u>.

When we realize that armed robbery and similar offences require the use of brute force, it immediately becomes clear that these are offences almost exclusive to the masculine world. The offences are thus expound. Besides, the need to be physically strong and <u>agile</u> tends to exclude the upper middle age and the elderly; so, age is also a factor. Moreover, members of the working class, who at least have some financial returns to rely on, hardly ever have urge to resort to violence. This tends to limit violent crimes to the employed, poor and desperate males in their late teens, twenties or early thirties. Indeed, if elderly citizens are involved, they function as the barons, the financiers, who sit back a home while <u>they let loose the dogs of vandalism and death</u>. They provide the money and tools for the frontline criminals.

Similarly, drug pushing tends to be more prevalent among the weaker sex, especially ladies twenties. They are biologically more attractive, and hence more likely to made through the airports and border posts while hiding deadly stach of hard drugs within on or other of their bodily crevices. Again, if older citizens are involved it is more as the barons, shielding the carriers from prosecution if they are caught. So this is another crime that is largely sex-bound.

Punishments for offences limited to the citizens on the lower rungs of the socio-economic ladder appear to be harsher. So, robbery with violence attracts death, and pushing hard drugs attracts long jail terms. Meanwhile, pan robbery and large-scale fraud, offences with are invariably specific to the high-class officials, do not attract severe penalties. In deed, most culprits at this level mange to wriggle out of the net of the law.

There thus appears to be sufficient reasons to answer out of original questions in the affirmative.

(a) Mention any two yardsticks used by ht writer to categorize those who commit violent crimes.

(b) What two roles do the barons of the identified crimes play?

(c) Among what group of people are violent crimes most common?

(d) (i) Does the writer consider the punishment for the various crimes mentioned in the passage as fair?

(ii) Support your answer with a brief description of the writer's argument.

(e) They let loose the dogs of vandalism and death.

    (i) What figure of speech is the above expression?

    (ii) What does the expression mean?

(f) For each of the following words, find another word or phrase which means the same and can replace it as used in the passage:

    (i) Pertinent;

    (ii) Agile;

    (iii) Desperate;

    (iv) Prevalent;

    (v) Severe.

MODEL ANSWERS S.S.C.E. 1992 COMPREHENSION QUESTION.

a.(i) Unemployed, poor and desperate males ages between tens, twenties and early thirty.

(ii) Ladies in their twenties.

b.(i) They act as their financiers by providing money and tools for the criminals.

(iii) The help to shield the carriers (of drugs) from prosecution if caught.

c. Among males and females in their tens, twenties or early thirties.

d.(i) No, because it is limited to the citizens on the lower lungs of socio-economic ladder.

(ii) The writer 's argument is based on the fact that robbery with violence and drug pushing attracts severe penalties while pen robbery and large scale fraud offences do not attract such serious penalties due to the socio-economic bearing of the culprits.

e. "..they let loss the dogs of vandalism and death".

   (i) Metaphor

   (ii) It means that they unleash untold danger to the populace.

f. (i) Pertinent - Relevant

  (ii) Agile - Desperate

  (iii) Desperate - strong willed

 (iv) Prevalent - common

  (v) Severe - serious

QUESTION 8

Read the following passage carefully and answer the question on it.

Marriage as a human institution is facing its greatest threat ever in the twentieth century. Never, since the first man and woman were joined together, has the institution been beset by as many problems as it is now. And this trend, which started in the Western World, has spread and is spreading to all parts of the globe.

The most disturbing problems is the high rate of divorce. It is no longer social stigma for women to fill the forms indicating that they are divorced; men too, proclaim their liberty from the shackles matrimony somehow with pride. Little wonder that young couples resort to separation and eventually divorce, at the slightest disagreement.

The availability of an alternative aggravates the seriousness of the problem. Instead of entering into matrimony, very many couples simple decide to live together. Even the courts now recognize such common law marriages, and respect the rights of partners in such associations, the case with which one or both can call off the union.

Besides, very many countries now enact laws that recognize the rights of children born out of wedlock. This singular factor has help to shoot up the number of such children in many civilized communities. A recent survey in an urban college shows that about forty per cent of eh students were born out of wedlock.

Not less among the factors hastening the death of he marriage institution is the progressively rising cost of living. Nowadays, it is essential for both partners to be gainfully employed to be sure of a reasonably decent level of existence. The marriage ceremony itself cost so much that the young men save towards it for years. Little wonder, then, that may young men simple remain single, raising one or two children from ladies <u>who themselves are often willing collaborators against the institution of marriage.</u>

(a) What does the author mean by referring to marriage as an institution.

(b) What do the words liberty and shackles mean, as used in the passage?

(c) (i) What, according to the passage, is a common-law marriage?

　　(ii) Mention one advantage of this system.

(d) Mention any two factors that are seriously threatening the marriage institution.

(e) Who themselves are willing collaborators against the institution of marriage.

　　(i) What is the grammatical term used to describe the above expression as used in the passage.

　　(ii) What is its function?

f. For each of the following, find another word or phrase that means the same and which replace it as used in the passage.

　　(i) Globe

　　(ii) Stigma

　　(iii) On alternative;

(iv) Enact

(v) Survey

QUESTION 8:

a. The author refers to marriage as an institution because, he sees marriage as matrimonial association of partners under law.

b. Freedom and bondage

c. (i) Common law according to the passage means that "very many couple simply decide to live together".

(ii) It allows for the fluidity of the association either of the partners can call off the union at any time he or she or both decide to.

d. (i) High rate of divorce

(ii) Decision of couples to just live together (common marriage law).

e. ...Who themselves are willing collaborators against the institution of marriage.

(i) Relative pronoun

(ii) Post qualifying the plural noun ladies.

f. (i)   Globe   -   world

   (ii) Stigma   -   mark

   (iii) An alternative -   choice

   (iv) Enact   -   promulgate

   (v)   Survey   -   research.

QUESTION 9   SUMMARY

MODEL ANSWERS

(a) Poverty and failure in one's life may come as a result of being born of a poor parentage, making of wrong choice in one's profession and associations, the inability to take chances in life and finally, lack of will power or drive in an individual.

(b) i. Most men remain poor as a result of their poor parental background.

   ii. Some men enter into the wrong profession and finds it extremely difficult to retreat.

   iii. Some men may associate theselves with the wrong associates that is wife or a business partner- thus bringing him down for life.

   iv. Some men lack the courage to take chances, thus ending up in poverty.

v. Some men regrettably lack the will power to further struggle to achieve success, they easily give-up after their initial trial or failure.

Finally, there is the will-power, most men are easily defeated by initial failures. They give up very easily. Lack of the will-power is the greatest enemy of success. Think of a man like Abraham Lincoln for instance, He failed at almost every human endeavour he tried his hand at –law, business, even politics. Undaunted, he tried the presidency. Not only he win, he is today among America's best known figures. He is one man who would have remained down there at the bottom of the pit had he given up.

(a) In one sentence, summarize the central idea of the passage.

(b) In five sentences, one for each, summarize the reasons why most men remind poor.

Then there is a factor of making a choice. Watch it, that man who appears to be an incurable failure at work may be lazy, my indeed be zealously hard working. His crime may be that he is in a wrong profession; he made a wrong choice. Some men are destined to be engineers, they went into music; some destined to be teachers, veered into medicine. Once a man becomes fully trained in a profession, he cannot beat a retreat. And he remains a hapless mediocrity in that profession.

Then there is also the factor of the choice of associate one cannot choose one's parents, but one can choose a wife, friends, business associates, and the like. This is where the mystery lies- you can make a choice, but cannot know in advance exactly how your choice will treat you. To choose a devil for a wife is to be sentenced to life-long anguish; the association will color every aspect of one's life endeavors, from education and social life to business. And to be yoked with an incurable fraud as a business partner may bring one down for life.

Of course, being is decisive too. To scale the begins demands courage, heights demands courage, being adventurous. One might be highly intelligent and particularly hardworking, but without the readiness to take chances, one's potentialities may never be given expression. Most of the paupers among us are, little more daring in taking advantage of situations around them.

QUESTION 9   <u>**SUMMARY**</u>

Read the following passage carefully and answer the questions on it.

I have thought seriously about it for long. Why do some people have to be condemned to the abyss of penury no matter how persistently they struggle against poverty? Come to think of it, there are so many physically agile men, well educated, with robust health, who eternally languish in penury's dark cell. And yet, there are others who, for doing next to nothing. Without taxing either their minds or bodies much, remain darlings of the goodness of wealth. In all my years of searching for an explanation, I have only a very weak solution.

Most men who are condemned to the chasm of destitution have their parentage to blame. This first factor is perhaps the harshest in deciding where a person belongs. To be born into a family of appallingly poor parents is to have to wage a losing battle against may wicked enemies. There is malnutrition to content with, and then comes illiteracy or poor education. With poor feeding and ignorance for ever trailing one, diseases soon catch up. And with these foes forever near, a serous pursuit of a meaningful profession can be rule out. One has fallen into the class of hewers of wood.

QUESTIO 8: COMPREHENSION PASSAGE NOV. 1992
MODEL ANSWERS.

a. (i) She was robbed of her much needed sleep/slumber.

(ii) One of her two bags was missing from the luggage compartment.

b. Her academic task ahead.

c. Trying to get some sleep, her mind keeps remembering her of her past experience.

d. She unconsciously fell asleep and in a dream sort of.

e. ...'When she got down'.

    (i) Adverbial phrase of time

    (ii) Functioning as a time adverbial "when" of the action "getting down".

f.   (i) Memories

    (ii) Meditated

    (iii) Bad experience

    (iv) Got down/dropped off

    (v) Shouted

QUESTION 8   COMPREHENSION

Read the following passage carefully and answer the questions on it.

Her first evening at the College of Education was eventful, not so much for what she did but for her <u>reminiscence</u>. She had traveled, all day long, from Ubeku, her village, to Lagos in a luxury bus. Most of the time the roaring engine had robbed her of a much-needed sleep. Throughout the journey, she <u>reflected</u> on her recent experiences with her male boss who got her sacked for refusing his advances. She surveyed the world before her, which held so much promise. Of one thing she was sure: she would not be found wanting in he academic tasks before her.

The noise would not let her sleep, much as she tried. So, by the time the bus arrived in Lagos, she was completely worn out, but was thankful that the ordeal was ending. It was then, when she got down, that she discovered that one of her two bags was missing from the luggage compartment. The bag contained some of her clothes, shoes, materials for make-ups, and the like. A very thorough search by the driver and other passengers yield no positive result. It had apparently been taken away by either an absent-minded passenger who had alighted before she did or by a thief.

The sleep that had been denied her in the bus continued to elude her in bed. Alone in her smartly painted, quite, and well-furnished room, she found her mind continually going on adventures into the past. In vain, she closed her eyes to woo the goddess of sleep; defiantly, her other self-re-enacted long forgotten scenes, until finally, a little before midnight, she found herself hand-in-hand with a man she had never met before. He was leading her to a beautiful garden with a quietly flowing stream in the valley. Somehow, though they did not speak to each other, their minds communicated, and she loved him dearly. But all this was before they got to the biggest part of the stream; there, the man suddenly pushed her in the water.

As she screamed, she found herself panting on her bed.

   (a)   What two losses had the lady suffered?

   (b)   '...The world before her, which held so much promise'. To what does this refer?

(c) Why did she remain awake for so long in the comfort of her room?

(d) What was actually happening when she found herself with a man in the garden:

(e) '...When she got down...'

   (i) What grammatical name is given to the above expression as used in the sentences?

   (ii) What is its function?

(f) For each of the following words find another word or phrase that means the same and can replace it as used in the passage.

   (i) Reminiscences;

   (ii) Reflected;

   (iii) Ordeal;

   (iv) Alighted;

   (v) Screamed

Question 7.

(a) The interviewer scores purely on impression given by the candidate rather than by carefully analyzed point.

(b) Subjectivity becomes a problem in oral interview as a result of self-comportment and appearance of the candidate or the candidates' readiness to talk freely.

(c) The mood of the interviewer's mood changes as the interview progresses.

(d) (i) The mood of the interviewer on the subject matter.

(ii) As a result of boredom on the part of the interviewer.

(e) ...Allowing them to influence scores"

(i) Adverbial phrase of reason

(ii) Qualifying the reason for..

(f) Assessing: scoring/examining

(ii) Weaknesses: inadequacies/fault

(iii) Woefully: terribly/regrettably

(iv) Athletic: sportsman-like

(i) What is the grammatical name given to the above expression as used in the sentence?

(ii) What is its function?

(g) For each of the following words find another word or phrase that means the same and that can replace it as used in the passage.

(i) Assessing;

(ii) Weaknesses

(iii) Woefully;

(iv) Aggravated;

(v) Athletic.

QUESTION 7:

COMPREHENSION

Read the following passage carefully and answer the questions on it.

One of the oldest and most often used methods of <u>assessing</u> candidates is the unstructured interview. It is called unstructured primarily because the interviewer scores purely on impression rather than by carefully analyzed points to be watched out for. Thus, the candidate is asked a series of questions and the interviewer awarded an overall mark according to his impression of the candidate.

The <u>weaknesses</u> of this method are apparent from the following paragraphs. In the first place, an interviewer cannot possibly avoid being subjective in his assessment. Perhaps he likes that appearance of the candidate or the way the candidate comports himself, or the candidate's readiness to talk freely. These are not the most significant factors in oral interviews and <u>allowing them to influence the scores</u> makes the assessment less valid. Secondly, where there are different interviewers, each one assessing his or her group of candidates alone, it becomes more difficult to arrive at a uniform standard of scoring. Each listener is impressed by different factors in the candidate's performance. Hence, it is quite possible for a candidate to score a high mark if he appears before interviewer A and to fail <u>woefully</u> if he appears before interviewer B.

Thirdly, even where only one interview is handling all the candidates involved, the uniformity of scoring is yet no totally guaranteed because the interviewers' mood is subject to changes as the interview progresses. The first candidate might be luckily purely because the interviewer is still fresh and is not bored by whatever the candidate says, whereas the last candidate might be unluckily because the interviewer may be tired, easily bored, and less interested in what he is being told.

Finally, the problem of achieving uniformity in scoring is aggravated by the fact that the questions thrown by the interviewer to the candidates are not usually the same. The interviewer may decide to ask a boy some questions on sport, while a girl is asked questions on domestic science. A candidate may indeed be unlucky to be faced with questions on a topic, which he cannot discuss at all. For example, he might be asked to discuss the game he likes best simply because he is <u>athletic</u> in appearance and the interviewer assumes he should be a sportsman whereas he cannot play any game.

(a) By reference, what is the basic difference between the structured and the unstructured interview?

(b) In what way does subjectivity become a problem in oral interview?

(c) Why may scoring be affected as the interview progress?

(d) Mention two ways in which a candidate may be unlucky in an oral interview.

(e) '...allowing them to influence the scores...'

MODEL ANSWERS TO THE SUMMARY QUESTIONS NOV. SSCE, 1990

a. (i) The speaker of the first variety of English finds internal interpretation from mother tongue to English language very lone and difficult.

(ii) The speaker, discussions with him is quicker and smoother save for occasional minor halting gaps.

(iii) The third variety speaker's thought is entirely English thus translation is not required, he exhibits his mastery of English language.

b (i) One can "graduate" from lower variety to the upper ones as a result of one's length of periods of education, exposure to standard English and finally through a personal conscious effort of an individual.

(ii) The switch from a higher variety of English language to lower variety, may be as a result of choice that is if one feels inclined to the lowest stratum of variety I if feel so inclined when discussing with a house-servant or a porter.

(a) In three sentences one for each, summarize the distinctive characteristics of the speakers of the three varieties of English described in the passage.

(b) In <u>two</u> sentences, <u>one</u> for each, describe the conditions under which a person can:

(i) Move from lower varieties to the upper ones;

(ii) Switch from a higher variety to a lower one.

COMMON FOREIGN UTTERANCES IN ENGLISH USAGE

It is usually a common place among intellectuals and academics, to blend their linguistic repertoire with other similar languages, which accidentally found themselves into English vocabulary. Albert, some of these languages especially Latin is no longer taught in most countries, nowadays, thus people refer to them as 'dead languages'. Nevertheless, one usually discovers that people (academics) still refuse to part ways with them, thus the need to study and know the meanings of the commonest ones among these foreign expressions.

An infinitum = for ever

The fans want the soccer to continue ad infinitum

Bona fide = in good faith.

She is a bona fide student of this great institution

He is a bona fide store man.

Carte blanche = freedom to do as one pleased in politics and in spending money i.e. He had to spend and spend, as his mother gave him carte blanche when he was going to the campus.

Soi-disant= self styled

Status quo= state of affairs as it is.

Tête-à-tête = Private conversation or interview

- Please come into my office for a tête-à-tête.

Vis-à-vis = with regard to

- The judge did not find the main guilty vis-à-vis the encounter between him and his landlord.

Ultra vires = Beyond one's power or authority.

- Because the judge acted ultra virus the case has been transferred to another court.

Vice verse = with the order of terms changed, the other way round.

- He called me names and vice versa.

Sub Rosa = in confidence

- She told me what happened sub rosa.

Inter alia = among others

- Peter said, inter alias, that he came into the yard and saw the thief.

In-to-to = completely

- The store was demolished in-to-to

interrorem= as a warning
- She told him his interrorem

modus Operandi = way a person goes about a task.
- the lawyer's modus operandi will soon be made known in the law court.

Ipso facto = by the fact itself; thereby
- This ipso facto, proves that the accused committed the offence.

mutates mutandis = with necessary changes.
- Everything will be right mutates mutandis.

noblesse oblige – privilege entails responsibility

nunodimettis = permission to depart (to sing nunodimittis
Means to be wiling to depart form life etc.

paripassu = with equal pace; simultaneously and equally.
- the two events occurred paripassu.

Persona non grata- A person, especially a diplomat, not accepted in a foreign country.

primus inter pares = First among equals
- Since all of them are graduates, whoever is chosen to head the school is just a primus inter pares.

sine qua non= something that one cannot do without

- Hard work is sine qua non for success.

esprit de corps = devotion to one's society or fraternity; team spirit

- Esprit de corps helps to promote the police force.

et cetera = and so on. He bought oranges, carrots etc

exampli gratia (e.g.) = for example.

- He said a lot of goodies e.g. that he will spray us with dollars during you birthday celebration.

ex gratia = done as a favor, not under compulsion.

- She did the work for me ex gratia.

ex parte = (used in law) = made or done in the interests of one side only in a lawsuit.

- He has obtained an ex parte order against eviction

ex-officio = by virtue of office

- The principal is an ex –officio member of the Ancopss.

Impasse = Dilemma, deadlock

- They have reached an impasse in their negotiation and there is nothing anyone can do now.

Habeas corpus = a written order requiring a person to appear before a judge or into a court to investigate the lawfulness of his detention in prison.

- They have applied for a habeas corpus so that the prisoner may be released.

Circs = about (with dates)

> The coup took place circa April 22 1991

Coup d'etat = the taking over of government by the army.

> Her campaigns for the deanship election were given the coup de grace when her close friends backed out.

de facto = in actual fact

de jure = law ful

- thedefacto owners of the oil field now are the Orumba family who have occupied it by force; but the dejure owners (lawful) are the Ekaetes who have been driven away from the land.

Deo Volente (other written D.V.) = God willing

- He will, Deo Volente, call on me, when next he visits.
- The birth day party will deo volente take place today.

Deus ex machina – power or event that comes in the nick of time to solve difficulty; provident and interpretation, esp. in play or novel.

en masse = all together

- we shall vote en masse.

www.ingramcontent.com/pod-product-compliance
Lightning Source LLC
Chambersburg PA
CBHW081348160426
43201CB00014B/2137